COMPUTE!'s

Kids
and the
Amiga

Edward H. Carlson, Ph.D.
Illustrated by Paul D. Trap

COMPUTE! Publications,Inc. abc
Part of ABC Consumer Magazines, Inc.
One of the ABC Publishing Companies

Greensboro, North Carolina

Printed in the United States of America

10 9 8 7 6 5 4 3 2 1

ISBN 0-87455-048-3

COMPUTE! Publications, Inc., Post Office Box 5406, Greensboro, NC 27403, (919) 275-9809, is part of ABC Consumer Magazines, Inc., one of the ABC Publishing Companies, and is not associated with any manufacturer of personal computers. Amiga is a trademark of Commodore-Amiga, Inc.

Contents

Advanced Programming

Appendices

Acknowledgments

My deepest thanks go to Paul Sheldon Foote for suggesting I write a book on teaching BASIC to children.

This book continues a series that started with *Kids and the Apple*. The Amiga is so different from previous computers covered in the series that I have extensively rewritten the material.

I helped prepare and teach in "The Computer Camp" summer camp at Michigan State University for these last four summers. I am deeply grateful to my fellow staff members at the summer camp: Mark Lardie, Mary Winter, John Forsyth, and Marc Van Wormer, all of whom shared their experiences with me and helped provide insight into the minds of the children.

Several families have used the Apple version of this book in their homes and offered suggestions for improvement. I especially wish to thank George Campbell and his youngsters, Andrew and Sarah; Beth O'Malia and Scott, John, and Matt; Chris Clark and Chris Jr., Tryn, Daniel, and Vicky; and Paul Foote and David.

I greatly appreciate the skill and energy of Stephen Levy in editing and assembling this book for COMPUTE! Publications, Inc.

Paul Trap shares the title page honors with me. His drawings are an essential part of the book's teaching method. I am grateful to Paul for his lively ideas, cheerful competence, and quick work which make him an ideal workmate.

My final and heartfelt thanks go to my wife, Louise. As absorbed in professional duties as I, she nevertheless took on an increased share of family duties as the book absorbed my free time. Without her support I could not have finished the work.

To the Kids

This book teaches you how to write programs for the Amiga computer.

You will learn how to make your own action, board, and word games. With them, you may entertain your friends and provide some silly moments at your parties.

Perhaps your record collection or your paper route needs the organization that your special programs can provide. If you are working on the school yearbook, maybe a program to handle the finances or records would be useful.

You may help your younger sisters and brothers by writing drill programs for arithmetic facts or spelling. Even your own schoolwork in history or a foreign language may be made easier by programs you write.

How to use this book. Do all the examples. Try all the assignments. If you get stuck, first go back and reread the lesson carefully from the top. You may have overlooked some detail. After trying hard to get unstuck by yourself, you may go ask a parent or teacher for help.

There are review questions for each lesson. Be sure you can answer them before announcing that you have finished the lesson.

MAY THE BLUEBIRD OF HAPPINESS
EAT ALL THE BUGS IN YOUR
PROGRAMS!

To the Parents

This book is designed to teach BASIC on the Amiga to youngsters in the range from 10 to 14 years old. It gives guidance, explanations, exercises, reviews, and quizzes. Some exercises have room for the student to write in answers that you can check later. Answers are provided in the back of the book for program assignments.

Your child will probably need some help in getting started and a great deal of encouragement at the sticky places. For further guidance, you may wish to read my article in *Creative Computing*, April 1983, page 168.

Learning to program is not easy because it requires handling some sophisticated concepts. It also requires accuracy and attention to detail which are not typical childhood traits. For these very reasons it is a valuable experience for children. They will be well rewarded if they can stick with the book long enough to reach the fun projects that are possible once a repertoire of commands is built up.

How to use the book. The book is divided into 32 lessons for the kids to do. Each lesson is preceded by a "Notes" section which you should read. It outlines the things to be studied, gives some helpful hints, and provides questions which you can use verbally (usually at the computer) to see if the skills and concepts have been mastered.

These notes are intended for the parents, but older students may also profit by reading them. Younger students will probably not read them and can get all the material they need from the lessons themselves. For the youngest children, it may be advisable to read the lesson aloud with them and discuss it before they start work.

To the Teacher

This book is designed for students in about the fifth grade up. It teaches BASIC and the features of the Amiga computer.

The lessons contain explanations (including cartoons), examples, exercises, and review questions. Notes for the instructor, which accompany each lesson, summarize the material, provide helpful hints, and give good review questions.

The book is intended for independent study, but it may also be used in a classroom setting.

I view this book as teaching programming in the broadest sense, *using* the BASIC language, rather than *teaching* BASIC. Seymour Papert has pointed out in *Mindstorms* (Basic Books, 1980) that programming can teach powerful ideas. Among these is the idea that procedures are entities in themselves. They can be named, broken down into elementary parts, and debugged. Some other concepts include these: "chunking" ideas into "mind-sized bites," organizing such modules into a hierarchial system, looping to repeat modules, and conditional testing (the IF-THEN statement).

Each concept is tied to the student's everyday experiences through choice of language to express the idea, through choice of examples, and through cartoons. Thus, visual and verbal metaphor is used in making the "new" material familiar to the student.

About Programming

There is a common misconception about programming a computer. Many people think that ability in mathmatics is required. Not so. The childhood activities that computing most resembles may be playing with building blocks and writing an English composition.

Like a block set that has many copies of a few types of blocks, BASIC uses a relatively small number of standard commands and statements. Yet the blocks can be formed into unique and imaginative castles, and BASIC can be used to write an almost limitless variety of programs.

Like an essay on "How I Spent My Summer," writing a program involves skill and planning on several levels. To write an essay, a child must organize thoughts from the overall topic to lead and summary paragraphs and sentences on down to grammar, punctuation, and spelling of each word in the sentence.

Creativity in each of these activities—blocks, writing, and BASIC—has little scope at the smallest level—individual blocks, words, or commands. At best, a small bag of tricks is developed. For example, the child may discover that the triangle block, first used to make roofs, makes splendid fir trees. What is needed at the smaller scale is accuracy in syntax. Here computing is an almost ideal self-paced learning situation, because syntax errors are largely discovered and pointed out by the BASIC interpreter as the child builds and tests the program.

On a larger scale, creativity comes into full scope, and many other latent abilities of the child are developed. School skills such as arithmetic and language arts are utilized as needed, and thus are strengthened. But the strongest features of programming are balanced between analysis (why doesn't it work as I want) and synthesis (planning on several size scales, from the program as a whole down through loops and subroutines to individual commands).

The analytical and synthetical skills learned in programming can be transferred to more general situations and can help the child to a more mature style of thinking and working.

About the Book

This book was written for the Amiga computer and was tested on a machine having 512K of memory, two disk drives, the color monitor, and version 1.1 of Workbench.

For instructors who feel themselves weak in BASIC or who are beginners themselves, the student's lessons form a good introduction to BASIC. The lessons and notes differ in style. The lessons are pragmatic and holistic; the notes are detailed and explanatory.

The book starts with a bare-bones introduction to programming, leading quickly to the point where interesting programs can be written. The central part of the book emphasizes more advanced and powerful techniques. The final part of the book continues building on these, but also deals with broader aspects of the art of programming such as editing, debugging, and user-friendly programming.

The assignments involve writing programs, usually short ones. Of course, many different programs are satisfactory solutions to these assignments. In the back of the book are solutions for assigned programs, some of them written by children who have used the book.

Lesson 14, "Saving to Disk," can be studied anytime after the first lesson.

Instructor Notes 1.   Windows, PRINT, BEEP, CLS

This lesson is an introduction to the computer. Your student may have many questions at the start, and you should pull up a chair and help in the familiarization.

The Amiga is a very powerful computer, but before you begin to see any results, you must go through a few setup steps. Stay with your student at least until the end of the first lesson.

There are instructions for every step, and several reminders that my experience with students indicates are helpful. But it is difficult to anticipate all the problems each new user will encounter. Every novice on a computer must practice and experiment until the ideas jell. More information about the use of the gadgets on the windows can be found in the manuals that come with the computer. There just is not enough room here to explain everything in detail.

Let's discuss the *enabling* of windows and *immediate mode.* When BASIC is first loaded from the Extras disk, you see two windows: a full-screen Output window and a half-size List window. The List window is enabled (what you type appears there). You must enable the Output window to do this lesson. Do this by clicking the left mouse button while the pointer is somewhere inside the part of the Output window that is showing. This puts you in immediate mode. The word BASIC becomes solid, and LIST appears in *ghost writing* to indicate the change.

If the keyboard locks up (the computer won't respond to any keystrokes) or if things seem to be in a hopeless mess otherwise, put the Workbench disk in and hold these three keys down at once: CTRL-Amiga-Amiga. (The Amiga keys have a large red *A* on them. One *A* is solid red; the other is outline red.) This restarts the system, but any program you had in memory will be lost. You have to reload BASIC from the Extras disk.

Some early Amigas were shipped with ABasiC instead of Amiga BASIC. This book treats Amiga BASIC, and some of the commands will not work in ABasiC.

The contents of the lesson:

1. Turning on the computer; the windows, icons, and the mouse.
2. The Kickstart, Workbench, and Extras disks.
3. Typing versus entering statements or lines.
4. Input cursor.
5. Enabling a window.
6. The computer understands only a limited number of instructions.
7. Statements: PRINT, BEEP, CLS.
8. Special keys: RETURN, SHIFT, BACK SPACE, CAPS LOCK.

At first, we use the two BASIC windows in their original locations and sizes. In a later lesson, we expand the List window to cover the full screen.

It is important not to remove a disk from the slot while the red disk drive light is on. You may ruin the disk. Likewise, do not click the mouse buttons while the disk drive light is on. It may crash the computer. This will not damage anything permanently, but will require you to restart the computer. You will lose any program in memory. When you turn off the computer, pause at least ten seconds before turning it on again. Otherwise, the computer may suffer electronic damage.

Questions
1. Show how to load BASIC from its disk.

2. What is an *icon?*

3. Name the two different BASIC windows.

4. Use PRINT to write in the Output window.

5. How do you enable the Output window?

6. What does the cursor look like?

7. How do you clear the screen?

8. How do you make the computer beep?

Lesson 1. Windows, PRINT, BEEP, CLS

Put Kickstart and Workbench in Your Computer

Push the Kickstart disk into the disk drive slot on the front of the computer until it clicks and drops down. Turn on the computer. The red light comes on the disk drive, and you hear it buzzing. In a moment the screen will show an upside-down picture of the Workbench disk.

When the red light on the drive goes out, take the Kickstart disk out of the drive and put the Workbench disk in. Wait for it to load. When you see the Workbench screen, and the red light on the drive goes out, take the Workbench disk out of the drive.

A picture of a disk with the word *Workbench* is in the upper right corner of the screen.

A little picture on the screen is called an *icon.*

Open the Extras Disk

Take the Workbench disk out of the drive slot and put the Extras disk in. The drive starts, and in a moment the Extras disk icon appears in the upper right corner. It doesn't matter if the Extras icon is on top of the Workbench icon.

3

Move the mouse until the arrow is on the Extras icon. Quickly, click the left mouse button twice. Again, you'll hear buzzing, and the red light will come on. The disk icon turns black, and you see a little tan balloon with zz in it.

Soon the Extras window shows on the left of the screen. In it are some icons. The AmigaBASIC icon is a box with orange flow lines on it.

Load BASIC

Now move the arrow onto the AmigaBASIC icon and double-click the left mouse button. Black icon, buzzing, tan cloud, red disk light all show. In a moment the two BASIC windows appear. One says BASIC in ghost writing, and the other says LIST in dark writing.

The BASIC Windows

BASIC has two windows, called *Output* and *List*.

The window saying BASIC is called *the Output window*. In the Output window is written some information about BASIC.

You use the Output window to tell the computer what to do. Then the computer prints its answers in the Output window.

The List window is where you put the programs you write. The List window is half-size and is inside the full-size Output window.

Enable the Output Window

Put the arrow under the writing in the Output window. Click the left mouse button. The word BASIC in ghost writing turns solid, and the word Ok appears in the window. At the same time, the word LIST in the List window turns to ghost writing.

When you point the arrow in a window and click the mouse button, the window becomes active. When you make a window active, it means it has been *enabled*. Only one window is enabled, or active, at a time. The window that is enabled has dark writing. The other window has ghost writing. Whatever you type will show in the window that is enabled.

Below Ok in the Output window is a little orange line called the *cursor*. It means the computer is waiting for you to type in something.

Cursor means "runner." The little line runs along the screen showing where the next letter you type goes.

Typing

Type your name. What you type shows in the Output window. (If it appears in the List window, you have not properly enabled the Output window. Read "Enable the Output Window" above.)

Now press the RETURN key.

Oh-oh! Screen flashed yellow, the computer beeped, the cursor disappeared, and at the top of the screen, you see

Undefined subprogram

What is wrong? The computer understands only about 200 words, and your name is not one of them. Whenever the computer doesn't understand you, it prints an error message at the top of the screen.

Making the Computer Go Again

Put the arrow into the OK box at the top of the screen and click the left button. The computer prints a new Ok, and the orange cursor is in the Output window.

Command the Computer

You need to learn which words the computer understands.

The first three instructions you will learn are

PRINT, CLS, BEEP

Type: print "hi"

If you make a mistake, press the BACK SPACE key to erase the wrong letters. Then type the correct letters. (The " marks are quotation marks. To make " marks, hold down the SHIFT key and press the " key that is next to the RETURN key.)

Now press the RETURN key.

The computer obeys your instructions. In the Output window it prints

hi

Then it prints Ok, and the cursor appears to tell you that it is ready for another command.

The PRINT statement tells the computer to write something in the Output window. It writes whatever words are inside the quotation marks after the PRINT statement. (The computer doesn't care whether you type instructions in capital letters or small ones. If you want to type in capital letters, press the CAPS LOCK key once. The little red light on the key comes on, meaning that what you type will now be in capital letters. Press it again to go back to small letters.)

Type and Enter Are Not the Same

When we say *enter*, we will always mean to do these two things:

1. Type something.
2. Then press the RETURN key.

The Computer Beeps Like a Bird

Here is another statement:

Enter: beep

(Did you remember to press the RETURN key?)

The screen flashes yellow, and you hear a beep. (If you did not hear the beep, check to make sure that a cable runs from Audio Input on the monitor to the LEFT speaker connection on the back of the computer. Also check that the volume is turned up on the monitor.)

The Window Washer

The CLS statement tells the computer to erase the Output window.

Enter: cls

(Did you remember to press the RETURN key?)

The Output window is wiped clean, and the orange cursor line moves to the upper left corner of the screen. This position is the "home" of the cursor.

Assignment 1

1. Use the mouse to enable the List window. Then enable the Output window again.

2. Now use the PRINT statement to write your name in the Output window.

3. Make the computer beep.

4. Now clear the Output window.

5. Practice starting the computer and loading BASIC until you are sure you can do it correctly.

Instructor Notes 2. Programs, RUN, NEW, Strings

In this lesson:

1. What is a program?
2. Windows menu: Show List, Show Output.
3. Enable the List window and write the program there.
4. Automatic capital letters for reserved words in a program.
5. RUN to execute a program.
6. Using Windows on the menu bar to show the List window.
7. NEW to erase a program.
8. PRINT with nothing after it to skip a line.
9. Strings, characters, constants.

In Lesson 1, the computer executed instructions (like PRINT, CLS, and BEEP) in the immediate mode. Once the execution was over, the statement disappeared from memory.

A program is a list of statements kept in memory. You enter the statements in the List window. To execute the statements in the program, you go to the Output window and enter the command RUN in the immediate mode. After the program executes, you can then go back to the List window to add additional instructions or modify the program. At some point, a serious program is saved to disk, but we will not do that yet.

The NEW command erases a program from memory.

The BASIC menu bar has four menus. One of these, Window, is necessary to redisplay the List window after it is erased as part of the action of the RUN command.

As an alternative to using the NEW and the RUN commands typed into the Output window, you can use Start in the Run menu and New in the Projects menu.

Some students may become confused by the many options and actions available with mouse, keyboard, screen icons, menus, and windows. If so, it would be a good idea to do a complete review, starting at the beginning of Lesson 1.

The idea of a *string constant*, used in Lesson 1, is explained. The numbers appearing in a string, for example, "19", cannot be used directly in arithmetic.

Questions

1. How do you do each of these things:
   Enable the List window
   Make the computer beep
   Erase the Output window
   Erase the program
   Print your name

2. What is a character? Give some examples. What is a *string*?

3. What special key do you press to "enter" a line?

4. What does the computer mean when it prints Undefined subprogram?

5. Write a program to print FIRE and make the computer beep.

6. After you run the program, how do you make the List window show again?

Lesson 2.   Programs, RUN, NEW, Strings

What Is a Program?

A program is a list of instructions for the computer to do. The instructions are written in lines. Another name for instruction is "command" or "statement."

Writing a Program

Program statements must be entered in the List window. First, you must enable the List window. Move the arrow to the middle of the List window and click the left button. The ghost word LIST turns solid, and the orange cursor appears in the upper left of the List window.

Type this line:

print"hi"

What you type appears in the List window. (If you make a typing mistake, read the section "Fixing Mistakes" below. Then fix the mistake.)

Now press RETURN. The small letters of the statement become capital letters. But the "hi" stays as small letters. The words in capitals are *reserved words*, or *keywords*.

From now on in this book, all reserved words will be in capital letters and most other things in small letters. But you do not need to use capital letters when you type keywords into the computer. Let the computer do it for you.

Fixing Mistakes

The cursor is now below the P of PRINT. Use the mouse to move the arrow between the i and h of hi. Click the left button. The cursor jumps between the letters. (If a little orange box covers one of the letters, or if some other orange mess happens, move the arrow away, click the left button, and move the arrow back and try again.)

Now press the BACK SPACE key once. The h disappears. Type h again. Again you have "hi".

Practice moving the cursor between other letters, then erasing the letter to the left and retyping it.

The RUN Command

Notice that the computer did not obey you by printing hi. You must return to the Output window and enter the command RUN to make the computer execute the program.

We mean *execute* like the soldier executing the command "Left face!"—not execution by firing squad.

Move the arrow to the Output window and click the left button to enable the window.

Enter: RUN

The computer obeys the command by printing

hi.

The computer also erases the List window. How do you get it back?

Show the List Window

There are two ways.

Enter: list

or use the Windows menu.

To use the Windows menu, press and hold down the *right* (not left) button on the mouse, and you now see the menu bar at the top of the screen change.

Holding the right button down, move the arrow onto the word *Windows.* The word changes to orange on a black background, and some more words appear.

Still keeping the right button down, move the mouse so the arrow is on the words *Show List.* They turn orange on black. Then let up on the button. The List window will come back onto the screen.

You see that your program line PRINT"hi" is still there.

Assignment 2A

Practice moving back and forth between the List window and the Output window. (Enable one window, then the other.) Run the program several times.

A Longer Program

Enable the List window. The cursor is below the first line. Add two lines to your program.

Enter: BEEP
          PRINT"computer"

Now your program has three lines.

Run the program. (Remember: Enable the Output window and enter RUN.)

The NEW Command

The computer just executed your program. It beeped and printed:

```
hi
computer
```

Now let's erase the program so we can write another.

Enter in the Output window:

```
NEW
```

A large box flashes onto the top of the screen. It asks if you want to save the program to disk. Answer no by moving the arrow into the NO box and clicking the left button. Then enable the List window.

Printing an Empty Line

Enter this new program in the List window:

```
PRINT"Here is the first line"
PRINT
PRINT"Skipped one line"
```

Run this program.

The second line of the program just prints a blank line.

String Constants

Look at these PRINT statements:

```
PRINT "JOE"
PRINT "#s47%*$"
PRINT "19"
PRINT "3.14159265"
PRINT "I'm 14"
PRINT " "
```

Letters, numbers, and punctuation marks are called *characters*. Even a blank space is a character. Look at this:

PRINT "   "

Characters in a row make a *string*. The letters are stretched out like beads on a string. A string between quotation marks is called a *string constant*. It is a string because it is made of letters, numbers, and punctuation marks in a row. It is a constant because it stays the same. It doesn't change as the program runs.

Assignment 2B

1. Write a program that prints your first, middle, and last names.

2. Now add a beep before it prints each name.

3. Erase the program with the NEW command.

4. Write a program that prints three flying birds. (Make the birds with minus signs and the capital letter *O*. The minus sign is on the key above the P key.) Run it.

5. Now add to the program to make the computer beep after printing each bird.

Instructor Notes 3.   REM, SAY, TRANSLATE$, Editing Programs

In this lesson:

1. The REM for titles and remarks.
2. The CLS statement in a program.
3. Computer speech: the SAY statement used with the TRANSLATE$( ) function.
4. Editing the program; moving the cursor in the List window. The BACK SPACE key.
5. Moving and expanding the List window.

Whatever shows in the List window is the current program.

The program is organized as lines. In Amiga BASIC, line numbers are optional. Later, we will introduce this idea of numbering lines and line labels which are essential for GOTO and GOSUB statements.

REM as a remark statement can be a bit confusing to new students. It needs be distinguished from PRINT.

The difference between *command* and *statement* is hazy. Commands are used in the immediate mode (when the Output window is enabled). Statements are instructions put into a program. But BASIC really treats statements and commands the same. Most often, the RUN command is used in the immediate mode, and the PRINT statement in a program. But, as we have seen, PRINT can be used in the immediate mode, and it is possible to use such commands as RUN, NEW, and LIST in programs.

Using PRINT to draw pictures is demonstrated. It is better to draw some at the end of each lesson than to do a lot now. After Lesson 4, drawing helps develop line-editing skills.

By now the student should be familiar with the differences between the List and Output windows. So it is time to expand the List window to full size. This allows longer program lines to be used.

Questions

1. What is the REM statement used for?

2. What window do you look in to see the program? How do you make that window appear if you don't see it?

3. What statement do you put in a program so that it will erase the Output window?

4. How do you make the List window larger or smaller? How do you move the List window?

5. What statements do you put in a program so that it will say "I'm an Amiga?" What disk must be in the disk drive for this to work?

Lesson 3. REM, SAY, TRANSLATE$, Editing Programs

Enter **NEW** and enable the List window. You are ready to write a new program.

(Remember, you enter **NEW** in the Output window, then click the left button in the List window.)

The REM Statement

REM means *remark.* Use REM to write any notes in a program that can help the reader understand the program.

Enter:

```
REM I do windows
PRINT"Scribble on the Output window"
```

(Remember, you learned how to fix typing mistakes in the last lesson. Move the cursor behind the error in the PRINT statement above. Use the BACK SPACE key to erase the wrong letter. Then type the correct letter to fix it.)

Run the program. The computer ignores the first line because it starts with the statement REM.

The computer obeys the statement in the second line to print Scribble on the Output window.

The CLS Statement in a Program

Activate the List window, and add these lines to the program and run it:

```
BEEP
CLS
PRINT"Clean again"
PRINT"That's all, Folks"
```

The program again scribbles on the window. Then before you can even read it, the computer beeps and the CLS statement erases the Output window. Run it again.

The Computer Talks

Enter NEW and enable the List window.

Enter this program:

```
REM happy
PRINT "smile"
SAY TRANSLATE$("smile")
```

Run it. The Workbench disk has to be in the drive before you can hear the computer say "smile" out loud.

(If you do not hear the voice of the computer, turn up the volume on the monitor. Also check that a cable runs from the Audio Input on the monitor to the LEFT speaker socket on the back of the computer.)

Moving the List Window

Use the mouse to move the List window around the screen. Put the mouse arrow on the stripes beside the word LIST. Click the left button and hold it down. Now move the mouse. The window moves, too.

Move the List window to the upper left corner, covering up the word BASIC in the Output window.

In the last lesson you learned how to enable a window. Remember? To see all of the Output window, click the *right* mouse button, pull down the Windows menu, and then release the button while on the Show Output item.

Big Window

Now use the mouse to show the List window again.

We want the List window to be full size like the Output window. Do this:

Find the squiggle in the little *white box* at the *lower right* corner of the List window. This white box is one of the *gadgets* of the window. Move the mouse arrow onto this gadget. Then click and hold the left button down. Now move the mouse. The List window changes size. Pull the corner of the List window to the lower right corner of the screen. Now the List window is full size.

When you have two full-size windows, you can see only one at a time. You need to use the mouse and the Windows menu to switch back and forth between them.

Or you can make the List window any size you want, then move it wherever you want on the screen.

Picture Drawing

It's fun to draw pictures with the PRINT statement. Here is a picture of a car. Enter NEW before drawing the car.

```
REM $$$ Mercedes-Benz $$$
CLS
PRINT
PRINT" XXXXXX"
PRINT"XXXXXXXXXXX"
PRINT"  O            O"
```

Don't forget to put the spaces in the PRINT lines. They are part of the drawing.

Assignment 3

1. Use some PRINT statements to draw an airplane.

2. Show how to make the List window a different size and how to move it around on the screen.

3. What does the computer do (if anything) when it sees the REM statement? What is the REM statement used for?

4. Use CLS, BEEP, REM, and PRINT to draw three flying birds on the screen. Make each bird beep after it is drawn.

Instructor Notes 4. Rainbow Colors

In this lesson:

1. The COLOR and PALETTE statements.
2. Foreground and background colors.
3. Printing in three colors on a colored background.
4. Cursor keys, holding a key down to repeat, the BACK SPACE key.

In a later lesson, we will use 16 colors to do graphics and text. But the standard screens support only four colors in order to save memory. The PALETTE statement mixes the primary colors (red, green, blue) and assigns the resulting color to a color number: 0–3 on the standard screen (0–15 later). If you change a color mix while a program is running, then wherever that color is used on the screen, it immediately changes.

The COLOR statement assigns colors from the palette to two elements on the screen: foreground and background. *Foreground* is called *text* in the book and is the color PRINTED to the screen. If you change a COLOR assignment during a program run, the new text and background colors apply only to further text PRINTed. (The whole screen background will take on the new color if CLS is executed.)

Special keys explained so far: SHIFT, CTRL, RETURN, CAPS LOCK, the two AMIGA keys, and BACK SPACE. The four cursor keys (arrow keys) will be explained in this lesson.

ENTER is identical in results to RETURN. ALT will be used later to jump the cursor around in the List window. The number keypad to the right of the keyboard duplicates the number keys in the top row of the standard typewriter keyboard.

Holding any key down a short time starts the *auto-repeat* feature of the keyboard. This is very useful for making repeated characters, such as a line of characters or spaces in a line, or for moving the cursor fast with the arrow keys.

When changing a line or text—correcting an error, for example—the change is not permanent until the cursor has been moved off the line, either by pressing RE-TURN, or by using the mouse or the cursor keys. This is a rather subtle point—easily overlooked since the line may not appear any different with the cursor off it. (But if there is a reserved word on the line in lowercase letters, it immediately becomes capitalized when the cursor moves off the line.)

Questions

1. How many colors can you put on the screen at once? How do you make blue letters on a white background?

2. Show how the PALETTE statement can make a yellow color (red plus green) and put it in spot 3 on the palette.

3. What is a cursor? What is it good for? Demonstrate the use of the BACK SPACE key.

4. Have your student demonstrate how to edit a line. This includes using the arrow keys to move the cursor to the interior of the line, modifying characters there, and moving the cursor off the line to store it in memory. Also, show how to use the repeat feature of the keyboard.

Lesson 4. Rainbow Colors

The BASIC screen can show four colors at once. They are numbered from 0 to 3. Right now these colors are:

color 0   background   blue
color 1   text   white   (the colors of the typed letters)
color 2   black   (gadgets have this color)
color 3   orange   (the cursor has this color)

Text means the color of the letters you print. *Background* means the color of the screen where there are no letters.

The COLOR statement picks which of these colors to use for the text and which to use for the background of what you print.

Try this:

COLOR 0,1   This makes blue writing on white background.
CLS   This clears the whole screen to white.

The numbers in the COLOR statement have these meanings:

COLOR *text, background*

Try other color combinations like these:

COLOR 1,3
COLOR 0,4
COLOR 4,3

In fact, try every possible combination from 0,1 to 4,3. Just be careful to make the two numbers different, because COLOR 0,0 makes blue writing on a blue background, and you cannot read what it says. (What does COLOR 2,2 look like?)

Mixing Your Own Paints

The PALETTE statement lets you mix red, green, and blue to make other colors. The only catch is that you can have only four colors on the screen at once.

It's like having three paint cans, each with a primary color. You have a palette with room for only four splotches of color. Instead of a color name, each place on the palette has a number: 0, 1, 2, or 3. You take some red, green, and blue and mix them together for color 0, then you mix different amounts for colors 1 and 2 and 3.

(Later in the book, we'll see how to have as many as 16 colors on the screen at once.)

Try this:

```
COLOR 1,0           (This gets you back to white on blue.)
CLS
PALETTE 1, .5, 1, 1
```

This turns *all* the writing on the screen to light blue. It even turns the writing you already did to light blue.

Why? Remember that your last COLOR statement said "color 1 for letters, color 0 for background." You just changed color 1 to something with less red in it. So the writing looks bluish green.

Palette *color number, how much red, green, blue*

The amount of each color is a decimal number from 0 to 1.

The Pure Colors
Try these:

```
PALETTE 1, 1,0,0 pure red
PALETTE 1, 0,1,0 pure green
PALETTE 1, 0,0,1 pure blue (hard to read)
```

And these:

```
PALETTE 1, 1,1,0   red   + green = yellow
PALETTE 1, 1,0,1   red   + blue  = magenta
PALETTE 1, 0,1,1   green + blue  = cyan
```

What do you mix to get white? To get black?

Now make crazy mixtures like:

```
PALETTE 1, .7, .2, .1
```

When you get tired, put white back on palette spot 1:

```
PALETTE 1, 1,1,1
```

Rainbow Colors
We can choose any color for background and then print on it with three more colors.

Run:

```
REM Leprechaun Rainbow
PALETTE 0, 0, 0, 0
PALETTE 1, .7, .3, .1
PRINT
```

```
PRINT " Pot"
PALETTE 2, .1, .7, .3
COLOR 2, 0
PRINT "        of"
PALETTE 3, .1, .3, .9
COLOR 3, 0
PRINT "           Gold"
```

After running, you have to do four
PALETTE statements to get back the
usual BASIC screen colors.

The Arrow Keys Move the Cursor

You know how to move the cursor in the List window by using the mouse and
clicking the left button.

You can also move the cursor with the cursor keys. Find the diamond of four arrow keys near the right bottom of the keyboard.

These keys move the cursor. Press one. Hold it down. If you try to move the
cursor out of the List window, the computer beeps and flashes a yellow screen.

Repeating Keys

Hold down the *h* key. You see:

hhhhhhhhhhhhhhhhhhhhhhhhhhh

This works for most keys. Hold down
a cursor arrow key. The cursor goes
whizzing along.

27

Erasing Letters

Enter:

REM aaaaaaaaaaEOiiiiiiiiiiiii

Move the cursor between the *E* and the *O*.
Press the BACK SPACE key. It erases the
letter *E* that was to the left of the cursor.

Now hold down the BACK SPACE key.
The cursor goes whizzing off to the
left, erasing all the *a* letters and
dragging the right side of the line
with it.

Assignment 4

1. Add to the Mercedes picture of Lesson 3 to make the car two-toned in color.

2. Draw a large "smiley face" in three colors.

3. In the List window, type this line. Then fix it to read CAT.

   REM CAAAT

   When you are done, move the cursor to another line so the correct line
will be stored in memory.

Instructor Notes 5. The INPUT Statement

In this lesson:

1. The INPUT statement.
2. String variables and boxes in memory.
3. Error message "Redo from start".
4. The two hats: programmer and user.

This lesson is about the INPUT statement and string variables.

In the statement's simplest form, **INPUT A\$**, there is no message in quotation marks in front. This allows the student to concentrate on the central feature of an INPUT.

Similarly, we will give only the essential feature of each command for the whole of the introduction of the book (through Lesson 14). We want the student to see the forest before going into details. The statements required for interesting programs are:

PRINT		output
INPUT		input
GOTO	allows	infinite looping
IF		branching and decisions
RND		random numbers for games

The box concept is used to introduce string variables. For the time being, variable names are restricted to one letter. This allows faster typing.

The "two hats" of the student—programmer and user of the programs—cause much confusion at assignment time. PRINT is the programmer speaking, while the user can speak only when invited by an INPUT statement.

Questions

1. What does the computer put in boxes?

2. How does the program ask the user to type in something?

3. How do you know the computer is waiting for an answer?

4. What is a letter with a dollar sign after it called?

5. Write a short program that uses CLS, PRINT, and INPUT.

6. Are you in trouble if the computer answers with Redo from start after an input? What made it do that? What do you do next?

Lesson 5. The INPUT Statement

Use INPUT to make the computer ask for something.

Enter:

```
REM Talky-Talk
SAY TRANSLATE$("say something")
PRINT"type your answer"
INPUT A$
SAY TRANSLATE$("did you say")
SAY TRANSLATE$(A$)
```

Run it. When you see a question mark with the orange cursor after it, type hi and press the RETURN key.

The question mark was written by INPUT in the fourth line.

When you type hi, the computer stores this word in a box named A$. Later, the program asks the computer to SAY whatever is in the box named A$.

Run the program again, and this time say something funny.

String Variables

A$ is the name of a *string variable*. The computer stores string variables in memory boxes. The name is written on the front of the box and the string is put inside the box.

Rule: A string variable name ends in a dollar sign ($). You can use any letter you like for the name and then put a dollar sign after it.

A$ is called a variable because you can put different strings in the box at different times in the program.

The box can hold only one string at a time. Putting a new string in a box automatically erases the old string that was in the box.

Error Message from INPUT

Run this two times:

```
INPUT A$
PRINT A$
```

Try these answers:

```
hi
hi, there
```

Rule: Do not put any commas in the string you type in answer to the computer.

If you accidentally do put one in, the computer will answer

```
?Redo from start
```

and wait. This means that the computer wants you to try again, but do not put any commas in the answer you type.

You Wear Two Hats—User and Programmer

You are a *programmer* when you write a program. The person who runs the program is a *user*.

Of course, if you run your *own* program, then you are the user.

When the programmer writes a PRINT statement, the *programmer* is speaking to the user by writing on the screen.

When the programmer writes an INPUT statement, the *programmer* is asking the *user* to say something to the computer.

It is like a game of "May I?" The only time the user gets to say something is when the programmer allows it by writing an INPUT statement in the program.

Assignment 5

1. Write a program that asks for a person's name and then says something silly to the person by name.

2. Write a program that asks you to INPUT your favorite color and put it in a box called C$. Then the program asks your favorite animal and puts this in box C$, too. Have the program print C$. What will be printed? Run the program and see if you are right.

Instructor Notes 6. Tricks with Print

In this lesson:

1. PRINT with a semicolon at the end.
2. PRINT with semicolons between items.
3. PRINT with a comma between items.
4. The "invisible" PRINT cursor.
5. Stepping through the program with the Outline A and T keys.

This lesson introduces the PRINT cursor which is invisible on the Output window. It marks the spot where PRINT will put the next character on the screen. (The input cursor is the flashing line.)

When a PRINT statement ends with a semicolon, the PRINT cursor remains in place. The next PRINT will put its first character exactly in the spot following the last character printed by the current PRINT statement.

Without a semicolon at the end, the PRINT statement will advance the PRINT cursor to the beginning of the next line as its last official act.

A PRINT statement can print several items: a mixture of string and numeric constants, variables, and the values of expressions. Numeric constants and variables have not yet been introduced. The items are separated by semicolons or commas.

If commas are used, the items will be printed in columns.

The series of printed items will have their characters in contact. If spaces are desired, as in the "toast and jam" example, the spaces have to be put in the strings explicitly.

You can single-step through a program using the Outline A Amiga key and the T key. The computer executes one statement at a time and, in the List window, draws a box around the statement that was just executed. In order for this to be done conveniently, the List window must be half-size or smaller. It should be located on the right of the Output window so that you can see the output and the list at the same time.

Questions

1. Which cursor is a little flashing line? What puts it on the screen?

2. Which cursor is invisible? What statement uses it?

3. How do you make two PRINT statements print on the same line?

4. Will these two words have a space between them when run?

    10 PRINT "hi";"there!"

    If not, how do you put a space between them?

Lesson 6. Tricks with Print

Enter this program:

```
REM food
PRINT
PRINT "toast"
PRINT "and"
PRINT "jam"
```

Run it. Each PRINT statement prints a separate line.

Now change the lines so the program looks like this:

```
PRINT "toast ";
PRINT "and ";
PRINT "jam"
```

Be careful to put the space at the end of "toast " and at the end of "and " and the semicolon at the end of each line.

Run it.

What was different from the first time?

The Hidden Cursor

Remember the orange line? It is the input cursor and shows where the next letter will appear on the screen when you type.

The PRINT statement also has a cursor, but it is invisible. It marks where the next letter will appear when the computer is printing.

Rule: The semicolon makes the invisible PRINT cursor wait in place on the screen. The next PRINT statement adds on to what has already been written on the same line.

36

Squashed Together or Spread Out?

Enter NEW, then try this:

PRINT "rock";"and";"roll"

After you have run it, try also:

PRINT "rock","and","roll"
PRINT "fancy","and","plain"

The comma in the PRINT statement separates items into columns.

Famous Pairs

Enter and run:

```
REM famous
SAY TRANSLATE$("enter a name")
INPUT A$
SAY TRANSLATE$("enter another")
INPUT B$
CLS
PRINT "Presenting that famous twosome:"
PRINT
PRINT A$;" and ";B$
```

Be sure to put a space before and after the " and ".

One Step at a Time

Find the two A keys next to the space bar on the Amiga keyboard. Both are red, but one is solid red and the other is outline red. Let's call them the Solid A and Outline A keys. In a moment you will use the Outline A key.

Enter:

```
REM steps
PRINT"first step"
BEEP
PRINT"second step"
CLS
PRINT"last step"
```

We need to see the Output window and a small List window at the same time. Click in the List window to enable it (so the word LIST is solid, but BASIC in the Output window is written in ghost letters).

Now we will *single-step* through the program. Hold down the Outline A key and press the T key. Whenever you're to do this, we will say "press A-T."

You see an orange box around the first line of the program.

Press A-T again. You see the box move to the second line. And in the Output window, you see the results. The computer prints

first step

Press A-T again. The box moves down one line and the computer beeps.

Keep pressing A-T until the program is done.

Every time you press the A-T keys, the computer takes another step through the program.

Assignment 6

1. Write a program that asks for the name of a musical group and one of their tunes. Then using just one PRINT statement, print the group name and the tune name, with the word *plays* in between.

2. Do the same, but use three PRINT statements to print on one line.

3. Single-step through your program using the Outline A and the T keys.

Instructor Notes 7. The LET Statement

In this lesson:

1. The LET statement used with strings.
2. The box model for storing variables in memory.
3. Distinguishing the value and the name of a variable.
4. "Taking" a variable from a box is really taking a copy.
5. Concatenation of strings, called "gluing" in this book.
6. Numbering lines.

The concept of memory boxes is used to introduce the LET statement.

The box model emphasizes that LET is a replacement statement, *not* an equal relationship in the sense used in arithmetic.

The box idea nicely separates the concepts *name* of the variable and *value* of the variable. The name is on the label of the box; the value is inside. The contents of the box may be removed for use, and new contents can be inserted. More exactly, a copy of the contents is made and used when a variable is used, while the original contents remain intact. When LET puts new contents in a box, the old contents are automatically erased first.

In this book, concatenation of two strings to make a longer string, using the plus (+) sign, is called "gluing" the strings.

Many forms of BASIC require that all statement lines in a program begin with a number. As you have seen, line numbering is optional in Amiga BASIC. In addition, you can give names, or *labels*, to lines. Labels will be introduced in Lesson 8 and will be used more often than numbered lines.

Questions
1. LET puts things in boxes. So does INPUT. How are they different?

2. In the program below, what is "MOM" called? What is the name of the string variable in this program? What is the value of the string variable after the program runs?

LET Q$ = "MOM"

3. What is in each box after this program runs?

LET A$ = "fat"
LET K$ = " sausage"
LET P$ = A$ + K$

Lesson 7. The LET Statement

The LET statement puts things in boxes. Enter and run:

```
1 REM in the box
2 CLS
3 LET W$="truck"
4 PRINT W$
```

Here is what the computer does:

Line 1   The title of the program. The computer ignores it.

Line 2   The computer clears the screen.

Line 3   It sees that a box named W$ is needed. It looks in its memory for this box. It doesn't find the box because W$ has not been used in this program before. So it takes an empty box and writes W$ on the front and then puts the string "truck" in it.

Line 4   The computer sees that it must print whatever is in box W$. It goes to the box and makes a copy of the string "truck" that it finds there. It puts the copy on the screen. The string "truck" is still in box W$.

Numbered Lines

In the "box" program above, each program line started with a number. Amiga BASIC lets you do this if you like. It helps when you want to talk about each line of a program.

Names and Values

This line makes a string variable:

LET W$ = "MOPSEY"

The name of the variable is W$.

The value of the variable is put in the box.

In this line, the value of W$ is "MOPSEY".

Another Example

Enter and run:

```
1 REM hungry
2 LET D$="pickles"
3 LET A$=" and "
4 PRINT "what goes with pickles?"
5 INPUT Z$
6 CLS
7 PRINT D$;A$;Z$
```

Explain what the computer does in each line:

1 _____

2 _____

3 _____

4 _____

5 _____

6 _____

7 _____

Gluing the Strings

Here is how to stick two strings together to make a longer string. Enter:

```
1 REM funny, funny
2 LET W$="har de "
3 LET X$="har "
4 LET L$=W$ + X$
5 SAY TRANSLATE$(L$)
6 LET L$=L$ + X$
7 SAY TRANSLATE$(L$)
```

Before you run this program, try to guess what the computer will say at line 5 and at line 7:

5 _____

7 _____

Now run the program to see if you were right.

Rule: The plus (+) sign sticks two strings together.

Assignment 7

1. Write your own program that uses the LET statement and explain how it stores things in boxes.

2. Write a program that inputs two strings, glues them together, and then prints or speaks them.

Instructor Notes 8. The GOTO Statement and the CTRL-C Keys

In this lesson:

1. Labels instead of line numbers.
2. The GOTO statement.
3. Using the CTRL-C keys to stop a running program.
4. Jumping forward.
5. Jumping backward and infinite loops.
6. "Spaghetti" programming.

The GOTO statement allows loops that go on forever. It also helps in the flow of statement execution once we introduce the IF statement. It provides a slow and easy entrance into the idea that the flow of a program need not go down the list of instructions.

For now, GOTO's main use is to let programs run on for a reasonable length of time. In each loop through, something can be modified. We'll use CTRL-C to escape the loop by ending the program.

Careless use of GOTO easily leads to "spaghetti" programming. Examples of spaghetti programs are shown. Although some fun is had with them, the idea is to make the student aware of the mess that undisciplined use of GOTO can make.

Lines can be named with a label, which satisfies the function that line numbers serve in other forms of BASIC. The label, always followed by a colon, can stand on a line by itself, or it can be the first element in a line (followed by the statement).

We now have three of the four major elements that lead to meaningful programming. They are PRINT, INPUT, and GOTO. Still lacking is the IF statement, which will change the computer from a sort of record player into a machine that can evaluate situations and make decisions accordingly.

Questions

1. When you run this program, what will appear on the screen.

```
        PRINT "hi"
        GOTO done
        PRINT "big"
  done:PRINT "daddy"
```

2. And this one:

```
  PRINT "Incredible ";
  here: PRINT "Amiga"
  GOTO here
```

3. How do you stop the program in question 2?

4. Write a short program that beeps, asks your favorite movie star's name, and then does it over and over again.

Lesson 8. The GOTO Statement and the CTRL-C Keys

Labels in Your Lines

Look at these four programs:

```
REM program 1          REM program 2
CLS                    CLS
PRINT "hi"             PRINT "hi"


10 REM program 3       sl:    REM program 4
20 CLS                        CLS
30 PRINT "hi"          last:  PRINT "hi"
```

They all run exactly the same.

Program 1 is the way we have written most of the programs in this book so far.

In program 2, we indented two of the lines.

In program 3, we used line numbers. You can use any integers (whole numbers) you want just as long as they are smaller than 65530.

In program 4, we used labels in two of the lines. The label is a single word followed by a colon (:). You cannot use *reserved words* like RUN, LET, PRINT, and so forth, as labels. There is a list of all reserved words in an appendix of this book.

Jumping Around in Your Program

Try this program:

```
REM whiz
    CLS
    PRINT "your name?"
    INPUT N$
loop:
    PRINT N$
    PRINT
GOTO loop
```

Run this program. It never stops by itself. To stop your name from whizzing past your eyes, hold down the CTRL key and press the C key.

The last line uses the GOTO statement. It is like "Go to Jail" in a game of Monopoly. Every time the computer reaches the bottom line, it has to go back to line loop and print your name again.

We will use GOTO in many programs.

More Jumping

Enter:

```
    REM shut up
    PRINT "say something"
    again: INPUT S$
    PRINT
    PRINT "did you say";S$;"?"
    PRINT
    GOTO again
```

Run the program. Type an answer every time you see the question mark and the input cursor. Press the CTRL-C keys to end the program.

Notice the arrow from the bottom line to line again. It shows what the GOTO does. You may want to draw arrows in your program listings.

Kinds of Jumps

There are only two ways to jump: ahead or back.

Jumping back makes a *loop.*

```
10 PRINT "HI"
20 GOTO 10
```

The path through the program is like this:

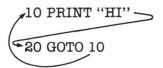

```
10 PRINT "HI"
20 GOTO 10
```

The computer goes around and around in this loop. Press CTRL-C to stop.

Jumping ahead lets you skip part of the program. It is not useful yet, but we will use it later when we learn about the IF statement.

The CTRL-C Keys

Pressing CTRL-C is a lifesaver. When you are in trouble, hold down the CTRL key and press the C key. The program will stop running, and you will see Ok and the cursor in the Output window. The computer is ready for your next command. Your program is still safe in memory.

In the rest of this book, we will say "press CTRL-C" as a short way to tell you to hold down the CTRL key and press the C key.

A Can of Spaghetti

Look at this:

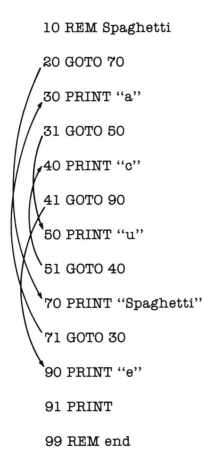

```
10 REM Spaghetti

20 GOTO 70

30 PRINT "a"

31 GOTO 50

40 PRINT "c"

41 GOTO 90

50 PRINT "u"

51 GOTO 40

70 PRINT "Spaghetti"

71 GOTO 30

90 PRINT "e"

91 PRINT

99 REM end
```

Whew!

This is not a good, clear program.

It is a "spaghetti" program.

Don't write spaghetti programs.
Don't jump around too much
in your programs.

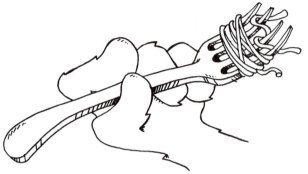

Assignment 8

1. Just for practice in understanding the GOTO statement, draw the road map for this spaghetti program:

```
REM Forked Tongue

GOTO s

n: PRINT "n"

GOTO a

s: PRINT "S"

GOTO n

e: PRINT "e"

GOTO whew

a: PRINT "a"

PRINT "k"

GOTO e

whew:
   PRINT "   B  i  t  e"
```

2. Rewrite the snake program above, leaving out the GOTOs.

3. Write a program that prints TEEN POWER over and over.

4. How do you stop your program?

5. Write another that prints your name on one line, then a friend's on the next, over and over. Sound a beep as each name is printed. Stop the program with the CTRL-C keys.

6. Write a program that glues two strings together and that uses each of these statements:

CLS, BEEP, PRINT, INPUT, LET, GOTO

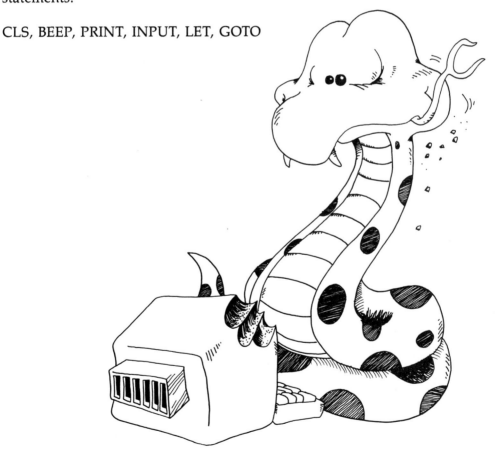

Instructor Notes 9. The IF Statement

In this lesson:

1. The IF statement.
2. Phrase A and statement C.
3. "If" in English.
4. "If" as a fork in the road.
5. The not equal sign.

IF is a powerful but intricate statement that is at the very heart of the computer as a logic machine.

The IF statement appeals both to our verbal and visual imagination. The "cake" cartoon and the "fork in the road" cartoon illustrate these ideas.

The GOTO statement has already introduced the idea that the flow of control down the program list may be altered. To that idea is now added the conditional test: If an assertion is true, one thing happens; if it is false, another.

Phrase A is used for the assertion being tested for truth. *Statement C* is used for the statement to be done if the assertion is true.

Two levels of abstraction occur in the assertions. On the literal level, we have the assertions *equal* and *not equal:*

A$ = B$

C$ <> D$

On the next level up, we have the *truth* or *falsity* of the assertion.

Some care may be needed to separate and clarify these notions.

When you see A = B, it may not *really* be true that A equals B because the assertion may actually be false.

The larger set of relations

| < | > | = | =< | => | <> |

will be treated in later lessons.

Questions

1. How do you make this program print THAT'S FINE?

```
start: PRINT "DOES YOUR TOE HURT?"
INPUT T$
IF T$= "NAH" THEN PRINT "THAT'S FINE"
IF T$= "NAH" THEN GOTO finished
IF T$<>"SOME" THEN GOTO start
finished: REM the end
```

2. Write a short program which asks if you like chocolate or vanilla ice cream. Answers to be C or V. For the C answer, print Yummy!. For the V answer, print Mmmmmm!.

3. What is meant by *phrase A*? By *statement C*? Where is the "fork in the road" in an IF statement?

Lesson 9. The IF Statement

Clear the memory and enter:

```
REM tell me
PRINT "Are you happy? (yes OR no)"
INPUT a$
IF a$="yes" THEN PRINT "I'm glad"
IF a$="no" THEN PRINT "Too bad"
```

Run the program several times. Try answering yes, no, or maybe. What happens?

yes _____

no _____

maybe _____

Two Parts

The IF statement has two parts:

IF *phrase A* THEN *statement C*

First, the computer looks at *phrase A*.

If it is true, the computer does *statement C*.

If *phrase A* is not true, then the computer goes on to the next line without doing *statement C*. It looks like this:

IF *phrase A* is true THEN do *statement C* and then go on to the next line

or

IF *phrase* is false THEN go on to the next line.

IF in English and in BASIC

In English:

IF your home work is done, THEN you may have some cake.

In BASIC:

IF a$ = "done" THEN PRINT "eat cake"

Assignment 9A

Clear the List window and write a program that asks if you like baseball or Monopoly. If the answer is baseball, the program prints play ball. If the answer is Monopoly, have it print something else.

A Fork in the Road

When the computer sees IF, the computer must choose which road to take.

IF *phrase A* is true, it must go past the THEN and obey the statement it finds there.

IF *phrase A* is false, it goes down to the next line right away.

Here is the road map with the fork in the road marked:

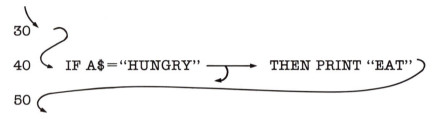

30

40   IF A$="HUNGRY" ——→ THEN PRINT "EAT"

50

The Not Equal Sign

=   means equal.

<>   means not equal.

To make the <> sign, hold down the SHIFT key and press the < key, then the > key.

Using the <> Sign

IF *phrase A* THEN *statement C*

Phrase A is a phrase that is true or false.

Choose this for *phrase A*:   b$<>"FIRE"

Put it in an IF statement:

IF b$<>"FIRE" THEN PRINT "Feed him hot chili"

IF   the b$ box contains "COLD"
THEN   b$ is not equal to "FIRE"
and   the expression b$<>"FIRE" is TRUE.

The computer prints Feed him hot chili

Or:

IF   the b$ box contains "FIRE"
THEN   the phrase b$<>"FIRE" is FALSE
and   computer will not print anything.

Here is how it looks in a program:

```
REM Old Smokey
SAY TRANSLATE$("With dogs it's a cold nose. ")
SAY TRANSLATE$("With dragons, it's.")
SAY TRANSLATE$("How is your dragon's brath?")
PRINT "(Enter 'fire' OR 'cold')"
INPUT b$
IF b$<>"fire" THEN SAY TRANSLATE$("Feed him some hot cheeli.")
IF b$= "fire" THEN SAY TRANSLATE$ "Watch out!")
SAY TRANSLATE$("Nice dragon.")
```

(Notice that *breath* and *chili* are misspelled so that the computer will pronounce them better.)

Assignment 9B.

1. Write a "pizza" program. Ask what topping is wanted. Make the computer answer something silly for each different choice. You can choose mushrooms, pepperoni, anchovies, green peppers, and so on. You can also ask what size.

2. Write a color guessing game. One player INPUTs a color in string c$, and the other keeps INPUTing guesses in string g$. Use two IF lines, one with a *phrase A*

g$<>c$

for when the guess is wrong, and the other with an equal sign for when the guess is right. The *statement C* prints wrong or right.

Instructor Notes 10. Introducing Numbers

In this lesson:

1. Numbers in PRINT, INPUT, and LET statements.
2. Arithmetic operations.
3. "Type mismatch" error message.
4. String and numeric variable names.
5. Can't do arithmetic (yet) with numbers in strings.
6. The equal sign is a replacement symbol, not an equality condition.

We introduce numeric variables and operations and revisit the LET, INPUT, and PRINT statements. The idea of memory as a shelf of boxes is extended to numbers. For the time being, we continue to restrict variable names to one letter.

The arithmetic operations are illustrated. The * symbol for multiplication will probably be unfamiliar to many students. Division gives decimal numbers, but since most arithmetic will be addition and subtraction, with a little multiplication, familiarity with decimal numbers is helpful but not essential.

Students may find it strange that the numbers in string constants cannot be used directly in arithmetic. Later in the book, we will introduce the VAL and STR$ functions that allow interconversion of numbers and strings.

You can print a mixture of string and numeric values by using a single PRINT statement.

The nonstandard use of the equal sign (=) in BASIC, that it means *replace* and not *equal*, shows up in such statements as

LET N=N+1

Questions

1. What are the two kinds of boxes in memory (that is, named by the kinds of things stored in the boxes).

2. Explain why N = N + 1 for a computer is not like 7 = 7 + 1 in arithmetic.

3. Give another example of bad arithmetic in a LET statement. Use the * or / sign.

4. Give an example of a program line that would have a **Type Mismatch** error.

5. Explain what is meant by the "name of a variable" and the "value of a variable" for numeric variables. For string variables.

Lesson 10. Introducing Numbers

Numbers in INPUT, LET, and PRINT

So far, we have used only strings. The computer can do arithmetic, too. Enter and run this program:

```
REM bigger
SAY TRANSLATE$("Give me a number.")
INPUT N
LET N=N+1
SAY TRANSLATE$("Here is a bigger one.")
PRINT N
```

Arithmetic

The +, —, and * signs are in the top row of the keyboard. The / sign is at the bottom, with the ? sign.

Computers use * instead of × for a multiplication sign.

Try this: In the bigger program above, change the LET statement so that N is multiplied by 5.

Computers use / for a division sign. Answers are decimals.

Try this: Change the LET so that N is divided by five. What do you say in the next line?

Arithmetic in the PRINT Statement

REM waiting
LET a=2001
LET b=1986
PRINT" How much longer, Hal?"
PRINT a−b;"years."

Variable Names

The name of a box that contains a string must end with a dollar sign. Some examples are b$, A$, name$.

The name of a box that contains a number doesn't have a dollar sign. Here are some examples: b, A, number.

The thing that is put in the box is called the *value* of the variable.

	Variable name	Value
LET a = 21	a	21
LET b$="hi"	b$	"hi"

Numbers and Strings Are Different

Numbers and strings are different. "1986" is not a number. It is a string constant because it is inside quotation marks.

Rule: Even if a string is made up of number characters, it is still not a number.

Some numeric constants: 5, 22, 3.14, −50

Some string constants: "HI", "7", "Two", "3.14"

There are two types of variables: string and numeric.

You cannot put a string in a number box or a number in a string box.

Correct: LET a = 10
Correct: LET b$ = "10"
Wrong: LET c$ = 10
Wrong: LET d = "10"

If you try to run one of the wrong lines, the computer will beep and print:

Type mismatch

To continue using the computer, you must click the left button in the OK box at the top of the screen. If you show the List window, you will see an orange box around the part of the program that is wrong.

Rule: You cannot do arithmetic with the numbers in strings.

Correct: LET a = 3 + 7
Wrong: LET b = "3" + "7"

Combinations

Try to guess what each of these statements will print. Then enter the line to see what happens:

PRINT 5 _____

PRINT "5" _____

PRINT "5+3" _____

PRINT "5"+"3" _____

PRINT 5 + 3 _____

Which of the lines above glues two strings? _____

Which line does addition of two numbers? _____

Which line just tells you about an addition problem? _____

Mixtures in Print

You can print numbers and strings in the same PRINT statement. (Just remember that you cannot do arithmetic with the mixture.)

Correct: PRINT a;"seven";"7"
           PRINT a;b$

Run this line: PRINT 5/2;"is equal to 5/2"

A Funny Thing About the Equal Sign

The = sign in computing does not mean *equal*. Look at this statement:

LET N=N+1

This does not make sense in arithmetic. Suppose N is 7. This would say that

$$7 = 7 + 1$$

which is not correct.

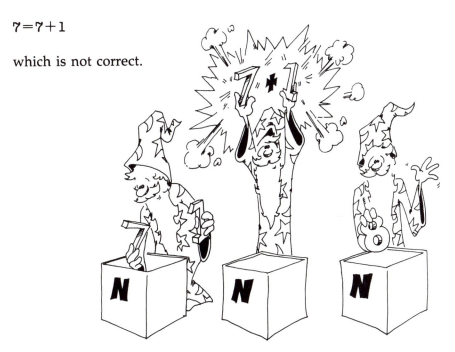

But it is okay in computing to say $N = N + 1$ because the = sign really means *replace*. Here is what happens.

Look at this: LET N=N+1

The computer goes to the box with N written on the front. It takes the number 7 from the box. It adds 1 to the 7 to get 8. Then it puts the 8 back into the box.

Another way to say the same thing is

10   LET   N   =   N   +   1

which means: LET (new N) equal (old N) plus one

Don't Be Backward

In arithmetic, you can put the two numbers on whichever side of the equal sign you want. But in the LET statement you cannot.

In arithmetic: N = 3   is the same as 3 = N

In BASIC: LET N = 3   is correct
                LET 3 = N   is wrong

In BASIC: LET N = B   is not the same as
                LET B = N   Why not? (what is in each box after each statement is run?)

LET N = B means _____

LET B = N means _____

Assignment 10

1. Write a program that asks for your age and the current year. Then subtract and print out the year of your birth. Be sure to use PRINT statements to tell what is wanted and what the final number means.

2. Write a program that asks for two numbers and then prints out their product (multiplies them). Be sure to use lots of PRINTs to tell the user what is happening.

Instructor Notes 11. TAB and Delay Loops

In this lesson:

1. The TAB( ) function.
2. Arguments in functions.
3. Delay loops: A special case of FOR-NEXT.
4. When numbers are printed, a space is put before and after them (the space before a number is really for the sign; therefore, negative numbers have a minus sign in place of the space).

The TAB function mimics the tab key of a typewriter.

TAB must be used in a PRINT statement. Several TAB functions can be used in one PRINT statement, but the arguments in the parentheses must increase each time. That is, TAB cannot be used to move the cursor back to the left. Later we treat the LOCATE statement which allows placement of the cursor anywhere on the screen.

Use of a semicolon between TAB and the thing to be printed is not always necessary, but is recommended.

The lesson discusses delay loops, which are useful in themselves, but are really just empty FOR-NEXT loops. Delay loops slow the program down so that its operation can more easily be observed. They also are called *timing loops*. FOR-NEXT loops are given as a unit, leaving an explanation of how they work for a later lesson.

Put the delay loops all on one line, with a colon to separate the NEXT statement. The amount of delay is determined by the size of the loop variable. A value of 2500 gives about a one-second delay.

After becoming acquainted with the primary effect of the loop—simply to count until a particular value is reached before going on to the next instruction—the student can more easily handle loops in which things go on inside.

Questions

1. Show how to write a delay loop that lasts for about two seconds.

2. Will this work for a delay loop?

   ```
   FOR q=1000 TO 5000
   NEXT q
   ```

3. Tell what the computer will do in each case:

   ```
   10 PRINT "Hi";TAB(10);"good looking!"
   10 TAB(5);PRINT "OH-OH!"
   10 PRINT TAB(15);"nope";TAB(1);"not here"
   ```

4. What is the *argument* in this statement:

   ```
   PRINT TAB(5);"E.T. call home"
   ```

Lesson 11. TAB and Delay Loops

TAB in a PRINT statement is like the TAB on a typewriter. It moves the output cursor a number of spaces to the right.

The output cursor is invisible.

The next thing to be printed goes where the cursor is.

Try this:

```
PRINT "123456789abcdef"
PRINT TAB(3);"y";TAB(7);"z"
```

Rule: After TAB(N), the next character will be printed in column N.

Careful! Try this: TAB(5)

You hear a beep and see Syntax error. You have to use TAB( ) in a PRINT statement. You cannot use TAB( ) by itself.

71

You Cannot TAB Backward

Try this:

```
PRINT "123456789abcdef"
PRINT "a";TAB(9);"b";TAB(3);"c"
```

The TAB( ) function can move the printing only to the right. You cannot move back to the left. If you try to go back, the computer prints on the next line instead.

Your Name Is Falling

```
LET n=1
PRINT"Your first name"
INPUT f$
again:
PRINT TAB(n);f$
LET n=n+1
GOTO again
```

Press CTRL-C to stop the run after your name disappears from the screen.

This program prints your name in a diagonal down the screen, top left to bottom right. Try other values of *n*. Try these changes:

```
n to 50   in the first line
n=n-1  in the next-to-last line
```

Fat Numbers

Numbers have a space glued on each side before they are printed on the screen.

Try this program:

```
PRINT "123456789"
PRINT 1;"a";-3;"b"
```

It takes spaces 1, 2, and 3 to print 1
      space 4   a
      spaces 5 and 6   −3
      space 8   b

If the number is negative, a minus sign (−) instead of a space is put on the left.

Functions Don't Fight, But They Have Arguments

TAB( ) is a function. Another function is TRANSLATE$( ). We will study other functions like RND( ), INT( ), and LEFT$( ). The number inside the ( ) is called *the argument of the function.* TAB( ) says "move the cursor over," and the argument tells where to move it to.

Assignment 11A

1. Write a program that asks for last names and nicknames. Then print the last name starting at column 5 and the nickname at column 15. Use a GOTO so the program is ready for another name/nickname pair.

2. Write an "Insult" program. It asks your name. Then it beeps, and writes your name. Then it TABs over in the line and prints an insult.

Delay Loops

Here is a way to slow
down parts of a program.
It is a *delay loop*.

Run this program:

```
REM Game
BEEP
PRINT "hide"
pause: FOR I=1 TO 9000:NEXT I
PRINT "coming ready or not"
BEEP
```

Line pause is the delay loop. The computer counts from 1 to 9000 before going on to the next line. It is like counting when you are "it" in a game of hide and seek.

Try changing the number 9000 in line pause to some other number.

Each 2500 in the delay loop is worth about one second of time. Try this:

```
REM tick tock
PRINT"Wait how many seconds?"
INPUT s
BEEP
many=s*2500
FOR t=1 TO many:NEXT t
BEEP
PRINT s;"seconds are up"
```

Assignment 11B

Write a "Slowpoke" program that prints out a short message with several seconds between each word. Have the computer beep before each word.

74

Instructor Notes 12.   The IF Statement with Numbers

In this lesson:

1. The IF statement used with numbers.
2. Nested IF statements.
3. Practice with < and > and <> signs.

In this lesson the IF statement is extended to numeric expressions. The logical relations used in this lesson are

$$= \qquad > \qquad < \qquad <>$$

It's a good idea to get the student to pronounce these expressions aloud. A < B makes a lot more sense when pronounced "A is less than B" than when it's just allowed to flow over the eyeballs. The points (the little ends) of the < and > signs point to the smallest of the two numbers.

We demonstrate the use of nested IFs. This powerful construction may be confusing. Go through the example to make sure the construction is understood.

A homemade loop is shown in the "Guessing Game." The IF at the end of a block of statements keeps the loop going until the condition G=N is satisfied.

Questions
1. What part of the IF statement can be true or false?

2. What follows the THEN in an IF statement?

3. After this program runs, what will be in box d?

    LET d=4
    IF 3 < 7 THEN LET d=9

4. Same question, but for 3 > 7.

Lesson 12. The IF Statement with Numbers

Try this:

```
REM Teenager
start: PRINT"Your age?"
INPUT A
IF A<13 THEN PRINT"Not yet a teenager!"
IF A>19 THEN PRINT"Grown up already!"
```

These IF statements are like the one that you used before with strings. Again, we have:

IF *phrase A* is true THEN do *statement C*

Phrase A can have these arithmetic symbols:

=	equal to
>	greater than
<	less than
<>	not equal to

Each *phrase A* is written with math language, but you should say it out loud in English. For example,

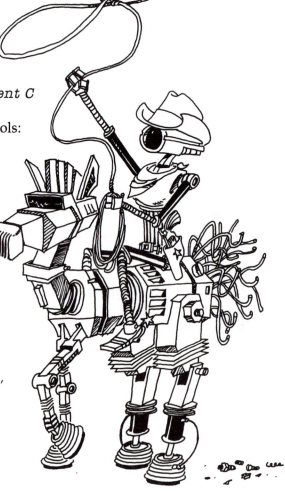

A <> B is pronounced
"A is not equal to B."

5 < 7 is pronounced
"five is less than seven."

Practice

For the following examples, LET A=7, LET B=5, and LET C=5.

Say each *phrase A* aloud and tell whether it is true or false:

A=B T   F   B=C T   F
A>B T   F   B<C T   F
A<B T   F   B<>C T   F
A=C T   F   A<>B T   F

An IF Inside an IF

The "Teenager" program above is missing something. Add this line at the end:

IF A>12 THEN IF A<20 THEN PRINT "Teenager!"

This is a nested IF statement. Break it into two parts:

IF A>12 THEN *(statement C)*   where

(statement C) is (IF A<20 THEN PRINT "Teenager!")

This line first asks, "Is the age greater than 12?"

If the answer is yes, the line gets to ask the second question, "Is the age less than 20?"

If the answer is again yes, the line prints "Teenager!"

If the answer to either question is no, the PRINT statement is not reached, so nothing is printed.

Assignment 12A

Draw the "fork in the road" diagram for the nested IF line above. There will be two forks on the diagram.

Guessing Game

```
REM GUESSING GAME
start:
PRINT"Two-player game"
SAY TRANSLATE$("First player turn your back.")
a$="Second player enter a number from one to a hundred."
SAY TRANSLATE$(a$)
INPUT N
CLS
SAY TRANSLATE$("First player turn around.")
guess:
SAY TRANSLATE$("Make a guess.")
INPUT G
IF G<N THEN SAY TRANSLATE$("Too small")
IF G>N THEN SAY TRANSLATE$("Too big")
IF G<>N THEN GOTO guess
over:
SAY TRANSLATE$("Congratulations. That's it!")
```

If you want to save this program on a disk, read
Lesson 14.

When the guess, G, is not equal to the answer, N,
then the computer says "Too small" or "Too big"
and goes to line guess again. But if G=N,
then none of the IF phrases is true, and
the program moves down to the last
statement and ends.

Assignment 12B

1. Tell what happens in each of the five lines from guess to over if G is 31 and
   N is 88:

   _____

   _____

   _____

   _____

   _____

   If G is 88 and N is 88:

   _____

   _____

   _____

   _____

2. Here is another program. What will it print, and how many times?

```
LET n=1
start:
IF n=13 THEN PRINT "unlucky!"
LET n=n+2
IF n<30 THEN GOTO start
PRINT "done"
```

   What will it print if the first line is changed to

```
LET n=2
```

3. Write a program that says something about each number from one to ten. The player enters a number and the computer prints something about each number: "Three strikes, you're out" or "Seven is lucky," and so on.

4. Add to the "Guessing Game" program so that it prints You're Hot whenever the guesser is close to the right number.

5. Add to the "Guessing Game" program so that it tells the player how many guesses it took to get the right one.

6. Write a game for guessing a card that someone has entered. You must enter the suit (club, diamond, heart, or spade) and the value (1 through 13). First, the player guesses the suit, then the program goes on to ask the value. Keep score.

Instructor Notes 13.   Random Numbers and the FIX Function

In this lesson:

1. The RND function.
2. The FIX function.
3. The RANDOMIZE statement.
4. The TIMER function.
5. Nesting function calls.

RND adds randomness in games and also helps make interesting displays like kaleidoscopes. You seed the random number generator with the RANDOMIZE statement and the TIMER function.

The RND function produces pseudorandom decimal numbers larger than 0 and smaller than 1.0. Such numbers are directly usable as probabilities, but integers in a specific range, such as 1 through 6 for a die or 1 through 13 for a suit of cards, are often more usable by students. The FIX function preforms the job of turning decimal numbers into integers.

The computer resets the RND function at the beginning of each run, so it will generate exactly the same set of pseudorandom numbers each time the program runs. This is usually awkward. We don't want an exact replay each time we run a game program.

The RANDOMIZE statement reseeds the pseudorandom generator so that each run of a program will produce different numbers. RANDOMIZE asks the user to input a seed number. To avoid this, just add the function TIMER after RANDOMIZE. This gives RANDOMIZE a seed number which depends on how long the computer has been on. That is usually sufficiently random to serve as a good seed.

After extending the random number to a range larger than 0 to 1, we often want to convert it to an integer. The FIX function does this by simply truncating the number—throwing away the decimal part.

For positive numbers, FIX works the same as the INT function which many BASICs have (including Amiga BASIC). But for negative numbers, FIX just drops the decimal part, while INT drops down to the next more negative number. FIX will round off a number if you first add 0.5 to it (-0.5 for negative numbers).

The concept of functions is again used in this lesson and is further clarified.

Nesting one function inside the parentheses of another is illustrated by using RND in the argument of a FIX function.

Questions

1. Tell what the computer will print for each case when g contains 2, 2.1, 2.95, 3.001, 67, 0 and 0.2:

   PRINT FIX(g)

2. Tell how the FIX( ) function is different from rounding off numbers. Which is easier for you to do?

3. Tell how to change a number so that the FIX( ) function will round it off.

4. What does the RND( ) function do?

5. How can you get random integers (whole numbers) from 0 through 10? (Hint: FIX(RND*10) is not quite right.)

Lesson 13. Random Numbers and the FIX Function

When you throw dice, you can't predict what numbers will come up.

When you deal cards, you can't predict what cards each person will get.

The computer needs some way to let you roll dice and deal cards and do many other unpredictable things.

Use the RND function to do this. RND stands for "random."

Run this program

```
REM Random Numbers
start:
LET n=RND
PRINT n
IF n<.95 THEN GOTO start
```

You see a lot of decimal numbers on the screen. The RND function made them.

Every Program Run Is Different

Run the program again. Notice that you get exactly the same random numbers the second time as the first time.

This is not so good. Each time you start running a game program, you want different cards or dice to show.

Here is what to do. Add the following line before start: in the above program:

RANDOMIZE TIMER

Run the program several times to see the different numbers with each run.

Bigger Random Numbers

RND gives numbers that are decimals larger than 0 but smaller than 1. To make numbers larger than 1, you just multiply.

Change the last three lines in the above program to

```
LET n=RND*52
PRINT n
IF n<46 THEN GOTO start
```

Run it again several times.

Now the numbers are between 0 and 52. They could be used for choosing the 52 cards in a deck.

But we want whole numbers like 7 and 23 rather than decimal numbers like 7.03 and 23.62. So we use the FIX function.

The FIX Function

FIX( ) takes the number in parentheses and throws away the decimal part, leaving an integer. Add this line before the PRINT n in the above program:

```
n=FIX(n)
```

Here is the entire program:

```
REM Random Numbers
RANDOMIZE TIMER
start:
LET n=RND*52
n=FIX(n)
PRINT n
IF n<46 THEN GOTO start
```

How It Works

Use this one-line program to see how FIX( ) works:

```
PRINT FIX(2.6)
```

Run it many times and try these numbers in the parentheses: 0.3, 0.5, 0.9, 1.0, 1.1, 1.49, 1.51, and 1.999. In each case, see that FIX( ) just throws away the decimal part of the number.

Rounding Off Numbers

Perhaps you know about *rounding off* numbers. If the decimal part starts with 0.5 or more, you round up. If it starts with 0.4 or below, you round down.

17.02	down	17
3.1	down	3
103.43	down	103
4.5	up	5
82.917	up	83

You round off numbers with the FIX function by first adding 0.5 to the number.

Run this:

```
REM ROUNDING OFF
start:
PRINT "GIVE ME A POSITIVE DECIMAL NUMBER"
INPUT n
IF n<0 THEN GOTO start
PRINT "ROUNDED TO THE NEAREST INTEGER"
PRINT FIX(n + 0.5)
FOR t=1 TO 1000:NEXT t
GOTO start
```

Try the program with numbers like 3.4999 and 3.5 and other numbers you choose.

Rolling the Bones

Generally, dice games use two dice. One of them is called a *die*. Here is a program that acts like rolling a single die:

```
REM ONE DIE
RANDOMIZE TIMER
start:
LET r=RND
PRINT "Random number";TAB(15);r
LET s=r*6
PRINT "Times 6"; TAB(15);s
LET i=FIX(s)
PRINT "Integer part"; TAB(15);i
LET d=i+1
PRINT "Die shows"; TAB(15);d
PRINT
PRINT "ANOTHER? <y/n> "
INPUT y$
IF y$="y" THEN GOTO start
```

What Goes Inside the ( )?

Numbers: LET X=FIX(34.7)

Variables: LET X=FIX(J)

Expressions: LET X=FIX(3*Y+2)

Functions: LET X=FIX(RND)

Here is how to save a lot of room.

Instead of this:

LET R=RND
LET S=R*6
LET I=FIX(S)
LET D=1+I

Use just one line:

LET D=1+FIX(RND*6)

Random Numbers in the Middle

Suppose your game has a funny die that shows only 6, 7, or 8 when you roll it.

Run this:

LET d=FIX(RND*3)+6

How it works:

Expression	Makes numbers from (small to large)	
RND	0.01	0.99
RND*3	0.03	2.97
FIX(RND*3)	0	2
FIX(RND*3)+6	6	8

Assignment 13

1. Write a program that "rolls" two dice, called d1 and d2. Show the number on d1 and on d2 and the sum of the dice. You do not need the variables r, s, and i in the program above. They were used to show how the final answer was found.

2. Write a "Paper, Scissors, and Rock" game, with you against the computer. (Paper wraps rock, rock breaks scissors, scissors cut paper.) The computer chooses a number 1, 2, or 3 using the RND function: 1 is paper, 2 is scissors, 3 is rock. You INPUT your choice as p, s, or r, and the computer figures out who won and keeps score.

Instructor Notes 14. Save to Disk

In this lesson:

1. SAVE, LOAD, FILES, KILL, and NAME commands.
2. Use only a backup of the Extras disk, not the original.
3. Put the disk's write-protect tab on "Write Enable."
4. SAVE overwrites the disk and LOAD overwrites memory.
5. When a program is saved to disk, the original is still in the computer's memory.
6. The "filename.info" files for Workbench icons.
7. Filenames can be 30 characters long and include punctuation.
8. Good filenames.

Refer to the appendix for making a backup of the Extras disk. Only the backup should be used in this lesson.

This lesson shows how to save programs to the disk and how to load them again.

Other statements and commands used in this chapter are

```
NEW REM LIST PRINT
```

This lesson can be used anytime after Lesson 3. Most of the programs up to this point were relatively short and uninteresting, not worth saving. The process of programming was being emphasized, not the end result of useful programs.

However, your own judgment should prevail. You can insert this chapter at an earlier point in the flow of lessons so that programs which your student is proud of can be saved.

You can use any mixture of capital and small letters for a filename. But when the computer goes looking for the filename you type in, it ignores the difference between capital and small letters.

Questions

1. What is a file?

2. How long can a filename be?

3. Can punctuation marks be in a filename? Can the filename have spaces in it?

4. How can you check that a program was actually saved to disk?

5. What happens to a program already in memory if you LOAD another program?

6. Does the filename have to be the same as the program name?

7. If a program is put into a file, is it still in memory?

Lesson 14. Save to Disk

If you already have a program in the computer, skip to "Saving a Program." If not, enter this program:

REM hi
PRINT "hi"

Saving a Program
Check that your disk is still in the drive.

You should not use the original Extras disk. You should always use a backup copy. There is always a chance that you can ruin the disk. *Be sure that you do not remove a disk while the red disk drive light is on.*

Check that the plastic write-protect tab is pushed away from the edge of the disk. It may say "Write Enable" or "Ok" in this position.

Enter: SAVE "hi"

You will hear a whirring. The disk drive red light goes on. When the red light goes off and the whirring stops, a copy of your program is stored on the disk.

(If the computer answers **Device I/O error** or shows a **Volume Extras is write protected** box, you may need to slide the little tab on the disk all the way down.)

Your original program is still in the computer's memory.

Easy Filenames

The filename of your program is hi.

We used the name hi because it is easier to remember if the file has the same name as the program.

If your program has a different name, save it again under the correct name.

The FILES Command

Let's see if the program is really stored on the disk.

Enter: FILES

After a whirring and the red light, you will see a list of all the files on the disk. Your file will say

hi

You will see another file called

hi.info

This file holds the icon for your file. You do not see the icon while you are in BASIC. It may appear when you use the Workbench screen.

Good Filenames

A filename:

- can be up to 30 characters long;
- is enclosed in double quotation marks (like "hi");
- can include numbers, spaces, and most punctuation in it.

A filename cannot contain a slash (/), colon (:), quotation mark ("), or an asterisk (*).

A short filename is best because there is less to type, but it should be long enough to make clear what is in the file. Try to use the same name that is in the REM in the first line of the program.

Good names:

L12 teenager
telephone list
tic tac toe
german vocab.

Wrong names:

CAT:DOG (has a colon in it)
a123456789b123456789c123456789d12345 (too long)

Loading the Program

Enter: NEW

Enable the List window and look at it. The List window is now empty because NEW erased the program from the computer's memory.

Let's get the program back. Enable the Output window by clicking the left mouse button while the mouse arrow is in the Output window.

Enter: load"hi"

You hear the whirring and see the red light, but is the program now in memory? Enable the List window to find out.

Erasing a File

So far, so good. But what if you change your mind and want to throw away a file?

Enter: KILL"hi"

And then enter: FILES

to see if it is really gone from the disk.

Oh-oh! Your file hi is gone, but hi.info is still there.

Enter: KILL"hi.info"

to remove this icon file from your disk.

Dangerous Commands
Careful: Both SAVE and LOAD are dangerous to your stored programs.

If you save a program to a filename you have already used on the disk, your new program will erase the one already on disk.

Likewise, if you load a program into the computer's memory, but you already had a different program in memory, the program you load will erase the one already in memory.

Renaming a File
You can change a filename with the NAME command.

If your file is named hi and you want to rename it hello, enter this:

NAME "hi" AS "hello"

Commands
These five commands are used with files:

SAVE *"filename"*
LOAD *"filename"*
FILES
KILL *"filename"*
NAME *"filename1"* as *"filename2"*

The Project Menu
Click the *right* button on the mouse, and pull down the Projects menu.

There are five items, and most have to do with files:

New	Like the NEW command, erases the program from memory.
Open	Like LOAD, lets you load a new program.
Save	Like SAVE, lets you save the program in memory to disk. It uses the filename you see at the top of the Output window.
Save as	Same, but asks for a different filename.
Quit	Lets you leave BASIC and return to the Workbench.

Assignment 14

1. Write a short program (four lines) and save it on the disk.

2. Enter NEW and write another short program. Save it.

3. Enter NEW and then enter FILES to see if the programs were saved. Load each program and run it.

4. Try out the KILL command on one of the programs.

5. Try out the NAME command on one of the programs.

6. Repeat the practice with the SAVE, LOAD, FILES, and KILL commands until you are sure that you understand them.

Instructor Notes 15. Some Shortcuts

In this lesson:

1. ?   Used for PRINT
2. LET   Omission
3. INPUT   Used with a message and with a list of variables
4. INPUT   Error message
5. THEN 33 Instead of THEN GOTO 33
6. :   Used between statements on a line
7. ′   In place of REM
8. Commands compared with statements

Now that we've reached RND and learned how to save programs on disk, all the elements are in place for the student to write substantial programs.

The colon is used to shorten and clarify programs by putting several statements on one line. A line should contain statements that have something in common.

The colon allows you to put a short subroutine consisting of several statements after an IF. This makes using a GOTO unnecessary for reaching the extended segment of a program. A shorter and much less cluttered program results. The colon then becomes a powerful and nontrivial means of improving the clarity of a program.

The colon can mess up a program, too. Be careful about adding other statements onto a GOTO, a REM, or an IF line.

INPUT followed by a message has two forms: If the message is followed by a semicolon, a question mark is printed on the screen; if the message is followed by a comma, no question mark is printed. In that case, you will probably want the message to end with a space.

Questions

1. What shortcut does a question mark give?

2. How can you tell that the word LET is missing from the LET statement?

3. An INPUT statement can have a message after it. Then what two punctuation marks can follow the quotation marks?

4. Why is it sometimes good to put two statements on the same line, separated by a colon?

5. What is wrong with each of these lines?

   ```
   10 REM beginning : GOTO write
   10 GOTO 50 : s$ = "Fast"
   ```

6. If the computer prints ?Redo from start after the user answers an INPUT, there are two things that could be wrong. What are they?

Lesson 15. Some Shortcuts

A PRINT Shortcut

Instead of typing PRINT, just type a question mark.

In the List window, enter

? "hi"

and press Return. The computer substitutes the word PRINT for the question mark.

A LET Shortcut

These two lines do the same thing:

10 LET A=41
10 A=41

Also these two:

20 LET B$="hi"
20 B$="hi"

You can leave out the word LET from the LET statement. The computer knows that you mean LET whenever the line starts with a variable name followed by an equal sign.

When the line starts with a name followed by a colon (:), the computer knows it is a line label. When the line starts with a name followed by a space, the computer knows it is a subprogram call (more in Lesson 21).

An INPUT Shortcut

Instead of

```
10 PRINT "What is your name"
20 INPUT N$
```

you can use

```
10 INPUT "What is your name";N$
```

Put a semicolon between the message "What is your name" and the variable. The computer prints a question mark after the message

What is your name?

and the orange cursor. Then it waits for you to enter an answer.

If you do not want the question mark, use a comma instead of the semicolon, like this:

```
10 INPUT "Enter your name ",N$
```

It is a good idea to end the message with a space if you use the comma.

Another INPUT Shortcut

You can INPUT several things in one statement. Put commas between the variables.

Run:

INPUT "Location"; X,Y

When you see: Location? on the screen, you enter two numbers with a comma between them.

Location? 5,6

Another example:

INPUT "Month, Day, Year";M$,D,Y

After the ?, type: September,29,1986

Error Message in INPUT

If you do not enter enough answers, or if you enter too many, the computer says

?Redo from start
?

and shows the orange cursor. You must enter all the things asked for, with commas between them.

Example:

INPUT "Month, Day, Year";M$,D,Y

?MAY,1
?Redo from start
?May,1,1987

Another Way to Get an Error Message
Run:

10 INPUT N,A$

Try these pairs of answers:

1, B
B, 1
1, 1
B, B

The error message ?Redo from start is put on the screen whenever the user answers a string for a number.

(It is okay to answer with a number for a string, because the computer says "Okay, 1986 is a string.")

A THEN Shortcut
Instead of

IF a=b THEN GOTO start

use

IF a=b THEN start

A REM Shortcut
Instead of typing REM, you can just type a single quotation mark (').

INPUT N$ ' The name of the user

is the same as

INPUT N$:REM The name of the user

A Colon Shortcut

Put several statements on a line with a colon (:) between them.

Instead of

```
Q=17*3
R=Q+2
PRINT R
```

use

```
Q=17*3:R=Q+2:PRINT R
```

When to Use the Colon Shortcut

Use the colon shortcut to make the program clearer by putting similar statements on the same line. For example,

instead of

```
X=0
Y=0
Z=0
```

write

```
X=0:Y=0:Z=0
```

The Colon After an IF Statement

You can avoid messy IF blocks by using colons.

Without a colon:

```
REM Guess
RANDOMIZE TIMER
g=1
a=FIX(RND*10)+1
```

```
guess:
INPUT "Guess a number from 1 to 10";b
IF b=a then right
PRINT "Sorry, try again"
g=g+1
goto guess
right:
PRINT "You got it in";g;"guesses"
```

With colons:

```
REM Guess
RANDOMIZE TIMER
g=1:a=FIX(RND*10)+1
guess:
INPUT "Guess a number from 1 to 10";b
IF b<>a THEN PRINT "Sorry, try again":g=g+1:goto guess
PRINT "You got it in";g;"guesses"
```

All the statements in the path a<>b is TRUE are on the line after THEN.

Careful: Do not put something on the end of an IF line that doesn't belong.

Example:

```
35 IF a=b THEN PRINT "Alike"
40 q=r
```

is not the same as

```
37 IF a=b THEN PRINT "Alike":q=r
```

because q=r in line 40 is always done, no matter whether a=b is true or not. But q=r in line 37 is done only if a=b is true.

Some More Mistakes with Colons

The REM and the GOTO statements must be last on a line. Anything following them is ignored.

Correct: p=3 : REM p is the price

Wrong: REM p is the price : p=3

Because the computer ignores everything else on a line after reading REM.

Correct: R=P+1 : GOTO 88
       here: S=3

Wrong: R=P+1 : GOTO 88 : S=3

Because the computer goes to line 88 and can never come back to do the S=3 statement.

Commands, Statements, and Lines

Commands and statements tell the computer to do something. The commands and statements we have used so far include:

BEEP, CLS, COLOR, FILES, GOTO, IF,
INPUT, KILL, LET, LOAD, NAME,
NEW, PRINT, RANDOMIZE, RUN,
and SAVE,

We have also used these functions:

RND, FIX, TRANSLATE$, TAB, TIMER

Statements are instructions to the computer which are usually used in a program. Commands are usually used alone in the Output window. FILES, KILL, LOAD, NAME, NEW, RUN, and SAVE are commands.

Assignment 15

1. Write a program that uses each of the shortcuts at least once.

2. Write a vacation program. It asks how much you want to spend. Then it tells where you should go or what you should do.

3. Write a crazy program that asks your name. The program has three funny ways of saying you are crazy. The program randomly chooses one of these and prints it after your name.

Instructor Notes 16. LOCATE and UCASE$

In this lesson:

1. The LOCATE statement.
2. Lines and columns in the Output window.
3. The UCASE$( ) function.

The LOCATE statement is used to move the output cursor to any point on the Output window.

LOCATE allows flexible manipulation of text on the screen and also allows a crude form of graphics made up of letters and other characters.

The full-size Output window is 61 characters across and 20 lines down. Remember the phrase "line, column" (which line down, which column across) to get the order of arguments in the LOCATE L,C statement. (We will find that the order is reversed when we get to graphics. There we need the phrase "X,Y" with X across and Y down.)

The UCASE$( ) function takes any string and changes all its lowercase letters to uppercase. It does not change punctuation or numbers. It has two uses. One is in making alphabetical lists. We will return to this in a later lesson. The other is in matching strings in INPUT statements. If you ask for **YES** or **NO** and get **yes**, you need to convert to uppercase before comparing the strings in an IF statement.

Questions

1. If you want to print the next word on line 12 at the left, what statement do you use?

2. If you want to print the next character on line 6, indented 20 spaces, what statement do you use?

3. How can you print **never again**, wait a second, then erase just the word **again**?

4. Show how to print the two words FAT and CAT on the same line with CAT printed first, starting at space 25, and then after a delay of about a second, FAT printed starting at space 5.

5. Show how to change the string d$="tiny letters" into capital letters.

Lesson 16. LOCATE and UCASE$

The LOCATE statement lets you put the output cursor anywhere within the Output window.

There is room for 20 lines of typing when the Output window is full height. The lines are numbered from 1 at the top to 20 at the bottom.

Each line can hold 61 characters when the Output window is full width. They are numbered from 1 on the left to 61 on the right.

Run this:

```
REM LOCATE
LOCATE 10,1:PRINT "line 10 first"
FOR t=1 TO 900:NEXT t
LOCATE 1,1:PRINT "line 1 next"
FOR t=1 TO 900:NEXT t
LOCATE 17,1:PRINT "line 17 last"
```

The first number in LOCATE tells which line the output cursor will go to.

Jumping Anywhere on the Screen

Run:

```
REM line and column
start:
LOCATE 1, 1:PRINT "Which line              "
LOCATE 1,13:INPUT L
LOCATE 1, 1:PRINT "Which column            "
LOCATE 1,13:INPUT C
LOCATE L,C:PRINT "*";
FOR t=1 TO 5000 : NEXT t
GOTO start:
```

Press CTRL-C to stop the program.

The second number in LOCATE tells which column the output cursor will go to.

Erasing What You Write

```
REM jumping here
again:
L=FIX(RND*20)+1
C=FIX(RND*58)+1
LOCATE L,C:PRINT "here";
FOR t=1 TO 1000:NEXT t
LOCATE L,C:PRINT "      ";
GOTO again:
```

How do you make the program stop?

The UCASE$( ) Function

Sometimes you want to make all the letters in a string into capital letters (also known as *uppercase* letters). The UCASE$( ) function does this.

110

Run:

```
REM ALL CAPS
again:
PRINT"Give me a sentence typed in small letters":PRINT
INPUT s$: PRINT
t$=UCASE$(s$)
PRINT"Here it is in capital letters:": PRINT
PRINT"     ";t$
ask:
INPUT"   Another <Y or N>";a$:PRINT
IF UCASE$(a$)= "Y" THEN again
IF UCASE$(a$)<>"N" THEN ask
```

Look at the last two lines. It doesn't matter whether the CAPS LOCK key light is on or not. The user's answer is made into a capital letter before it is tested against the "Y" and the "N".

UCASE$( ) is handy when you want to make an alphabetical list whose words contain both uppercase and lowercase letters. We will do this in a later lesson.

Assignment 16

1. Use the RND function to write your name at random places on the screen. Make it write your name many times all over the screen.

2. Use LOCATE to write your name in a large X on the screen.

3. Change the above program so that if you enter your name in small letters, it still makes the X in large letters. Use UCASE$( ).

Instructor Notes 17. FOR-NEXT Loops

In this lesson:

1. The FOR, NEXT, and STEP statements.
2. Values for the loop variable and for STEP.
3. Nested loops.
4. Skipping the loop if it is satisfied at entry.
5. Indenting loop interiors in the listing.
6. The Run menu.

A loop is made of a FOR statement (which may contain a STEP value) and a NEXT statement. These statements may be separated by several lines, and yet they are strongly interdependent. The student builds on the notion of a delay loop and learns the utility of repeating a set of commands in the middle of a loop.

Nested loops are introduced by using an example where the inside loop is a delay loop.

Amiga BASIC, unlike some other versions, detects whether the exit condition of a FOR-NEXT loop is satisfied before the loop is run even once. This makes for cleaner logic in your programs, but may show an unexpected bug if you copy certain non-Amiga programs into Amiga BASIC.

The FOR statement is evaluated just once at the time the loop is entered. It puts the starting value of the loop variable into variable storage where it is treated just as any other numeric variable. The STEP value, the ending value, and the address of the first statement after the FOR are put on a stack.

From then on, all the looping action takes place at the NEXT statement. Upon reaching NEXT, the loop variable is incremented by the value of the STEP and compared with the end value. If the loop variable is larger than the end value (or smaller in the case of negative STEPs), NEXT passes control to the statement after itself. Otherwise, it sends control to the statement after the FOR statement.

Because BASIC treats the loop variable just like any other variable, it can be used or changed in the body of the loop. Jumping into the middle of a loop is usually a disaster. Jumping out of a loop before reaching NEXT is commonly done, but in some cases (especially where subroutines are involved) may give hard to find bugs.

The Run menu is handy for starting, stopping, suspending, and continuing program runs. In addition, it lets you step through the program just as the A-T keys do, but it requires a lot of mouse movement. It is easier to automatically step through a program using Trace On from the menu.

Trace On slows the program down and also highlights the current statement in the List window with an orange box.

Questions

1. What is the loop variable in this line?

    FOR Q=1 TO 10 : PRINT T$: NEXT Q

2. Write a loop that prints the numbers from 0 to 20 by twos.

3. Write a "Ten Little Indians" program loop that prints from ten down to zero Indians.

Lesson 17. FOR-NEXT Loops

Remember the delay loop? The computer counted from 1 to 2000 and then went on.

FOR t=1 TO 2000:NEXT t

The computer is smarter than that. It can do other things while it is counting.

Run this:

```
REM counting
FOR i=5 TO 20
PRINT i
NEXT i
```

The loop can start on any number and end on any higher number.

Try changing the FOR line in these ways:

FOR I=100 TO 101

FOR I=-7 TO 13

FOR I=1.3 TO 5.7

Mark Up Your Listings

Show where the loops are by arrows:

```
REM on paper
FOR I=0 TO 7
PRINT I
NEXT I
```

STEPs

The computer was counting by ones in the above programs. To make it count by twos, change the FOR statement to this:

```
FOR i=10 TO 30 STEP 2
```

Assignment 17A

Have the computer count by fives from 0 to 100.

Count Down Loops

You can make the computer count down by using a negative STEP.

Try this:

```
REM countdown
FOR i= 10 to 1 STEP −1
PRINT i
FOR t=1 to 500:NEXT t
NEXT i
```

Nested Loops

In this program, we have one loop inside another.

The outside loop is FOR i ... NEXT i.

The inside loop is FOR t ... NEXT t.

These are *nested loops*. They are like the baby's set of toy boxes which fit inside each other.

Loop Variables

To make sure that each FOR statement knows which NEXT statement belongs to it, the NEXT statement ends in the *loop variable* name.

FOR j=1 TO 740 : NEXT j

Here, j is the loop variable.

Badly Nested Loops

The inside loop must be all the way inside:

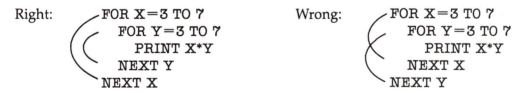

Right:
```
  FOR X=3 TO 7
    FOR Y=3 TO 7
      PRINT X*Y
    NEXT Y
  NEXT X
```

Wrong:
```
  FOR X=3 TO 7
    FOR Y=3 TO 7
      PRINT X*Y
    NEXT X
  NEXT Y
```

Don't let the lines connecting one FOR-NEXT pair cross the arrow of another pair.

Nonsense Loops

Amiga BASIC skips loops that are not supposed to run.

Run this:

```
1 REM nonsense
2 PRINT K
3 FOR K=5 TO 3
4 PRINT K;"Got here!"
5 NEXT K
6 PRINT K
```

This is a nonsense loop. The FOR statement says that K should start at 5 and get bigger, until it is larger than 3. But it is bigger than 3 to start with.

So you want the computer to skip the whole loop, jumping down to line 6. It does.

In line 2, it prints 0. This is because the variable K has not been defined yet. When a variable is used that hasn't been defined, it is given the value 0.

Line 3 sets K to 5, then notices that the loop should not run. So it skips down to the line after the NEXT, which is line 6.

Line 6 prints the value of K, which is 5.

The program never reaches line 4, so it never prints Got here!.

The Run Menu

Start	Same as the RUN command
Stop	Same as CTRL-C or the END statement
Continue	Same as the CONT command (Lesson 31)
Suspend	Same as the STOP command (Lesson 31)

Trace On (Off)   Used for debugging (an automatic version of Step)

Step   Same as the A-T keys (Lesson 6)

Enter:

```
REM stop
FOR i=1 TO 10000
LOCATE 1,1:PRINT i
NEXT i
```

Flying Boxes For Debugging

Remember the A-T keys that step the program along? (See Lesson 6.) The Trace On menu item does this automatically.

Start the program again. Using the *right* mouse button, select Trace On from the Run menu and then Show List from the Windows menu. The orange boxes start flying around the List window lines as the numbers print onto the screen.

Assignment 17B

1. Write a program that prints your name 15 times.

2. Make it indent each time by two spaces more. It will go diagonally down the screen. Use TAB in a loop.

3. Now make it write your name 20 times, starting at the bottom of the screen and going up. Use LOCATE in a loop.

4. Now make it write your name on one line, your friend's name on the next, and keep switching until each name is written five times.

Instructor Notes 18.   DATA, READ, and RESTORE

In this lesson:

1. The DATA, READ, and RESTORE statements.
2. Ways to put data into a program.
3. Pointer to items in a DATA statement.
4. Skipping items in DATA statements.
5. Why use DATA?
6. RESTORE the pointer to a given DATA statement.
7. Using quotation marks around data items.
8. Type mismatch error.

The idea of a *pointer* is used in this lesson. A pencil in the instructor's hand, pointing to items in a DATA statement, helps clarify this concept.

The DATA statement contains data items separated by commas. The items can be a mixture of string constants and numeric constants.

You put data in the DATA statement at the time you write the program. READ gets one data item from the DATA statement and advances the pointer to the next item. RESTORE puts the pointer back to the beginning of any designated DATA statement.

You can never change any of the data in the statement unless you rewrite the program. Of course, you can READ the data into a variable box, then change what is in the box.

You must READ the data to be able to use it. Normally, it is read in order. If you want to skip some data that is in a given DATA statement, you have to read and throw away the items before it. This procedure is illustrated in the program "Lots of data," where Sun and Mon are read and not used. Tu and Wed are printed.

In Amiga BASIC, you can skip data items by arranging them in different DATA statements, and pointing to the one you want with a RESTORE *NNN* statement, where *NNN* is the line label or line number of the DATA statement. This is especially handy in modular programs where several different modules have their own DATA statements. Each such module should start with a RESTORE to the start of its own DATA section.

You can read only numbers into numeric variables and string constants into string variables. However, remember that numeric characters can be put into string constants. An example is shown.

Questions

1. What happens if you try to READ more data items than are in the DATA statements?

2. What rule tells you where to put the DATA statements in the program? Where can you put READ statements?

3. Can you put numeric data and string data in the same DATA statement?

4. Can you change the items in a DATA statement while the program runs?

5. The idea of a *pointer* helps in thinking about DATA statements. Explain how.

Lesson 18. DATA, READ, and RESTORE

There are two kinds of data in your programs:

1. The data you INPUT through the keyboard.

```
REM First kind of data
SAY TRANSLATE$("Your pet peeve")
INPUT p$
SAY TRANSLATE$("Really! You do not like "+p$)
```

In this program, p$ is data entered by the user as the program runs.

2. The data that is stored in the program at the time it is written.

```
REM The second kind of data
X=57
Y$= "FLAVORS"
PRINT X;Y$
```

In this program, X and Y$ are data stored in the program by the programmer when it was written.

Storing Lots of Data

It is okay to store small amounts of data in LET statements. But it is awkward to store large amounts of data that way.

Use the DATA statement to store large amounts of data.

Use the READ statement to get the data from the DATA statement.

```
1 REM Lots of data
2 DATA Sun, Mon, Tu, Wed, Th, Fri, Sat
3 READ D1$,D2$,D3$,D4$
4 PRINT D3$,D4$
```

After the program runs, box D1$ holds the first item in the DATA list (Sun), box D2$ holds the second (Mon), and so on.

Strange Rules

1. It doesn't matter where the DATA statement is in the program.

   Do this: Move line 2 in the above program to the end of the program. Call it line 5. (Use the Copy and the Paste items in the Edit menu.)

   Run the program. It works just the same.

2. It doesn't matter how many DATA statements there are.

   Do this: Break the DATA statement into two:

   5 DATA Sun, Mon, Tu
   6 DATA Wed, Th, Fri, Sat

Run the program. It works just the same as before.

It Is Polite for the READ Statement to Point

READ uses a pointer. It always points to the next item to be read.

You can't see the pointer. Just imagine it is there.

When the program starts, the READ pointer points to the first item in the first DATA statement in the program.

Each time the program executes a READ statement, the pointer moves to the next item in the DATA list.

If the pointer gets to the end of one DATA statement, it automatically goes to the next DATA statement, farther down in the program listing.

It doesn't matter if there are a lot of lines between.

Do this: Move line 5 back to line 2. (Leave line 6 alone.)

2 DATA Sun, Mon, Tu
. . .
6 DATA Wed, Th, Fri, Sat

Run the program. It works just the same.

Falling Off the End of the DATA Planks

When the pointer reaches the last item in the last DATA statement in the program, there are no more items left to read. If you try to READ again, you will see an error message:

Out of DATA

Back to Square One

At any point in the program, you have only three choices for the READ pointer.

1. You can do another READ—then the pointer moves ahead one item.

2. You can RESTORE—then the READ pointer is put back to the beginning of the first DATA statement in the program.

3. You can RESTORE *nnn*—the *nnn* is a label or line number of a DATA statement. The READ pointer is put on the first item in that DATA statement.

Try this: Add a line after line 2 and run the program again:

RESTORE 6

This time the computer starts with data line 6, and prints

Fri Sat

Quotation Marks Around Data Items

String items in a DATA statement can have quotation marks around them.

Try this:

2 DATA Sun, Mon, "Tu"

Mixtures of DATA

The DATA statement can hold strings or numbers in any order.

But you must be careful in your READ statement to have the correct type of variable to match the item of data.

Correct:

DATA 77,fuzz
READ N
READ B$

Wrong:

```
DATA 77,fuzz
READ B$
READ N
```

You can't put fuzz in a number box.

Assignment 18

Write a program naming your relatives. When you ask the computer UNCLE, it gives the names of all your uncles. The DATA statements will have pairs of items. The first item is a relation like FATHER or COUSIN. The second item is a person's name. Of course, you may have several sisters, for example, each with a DATA statement.

Instructor Notes 19. Sound

In this lesson:

1. The SOUND statement.
2. Making the scale.
3. Setting the volume level.
4. Use of DATA to store notes.
5. Rests and tempo.

The SOUND statement produces a tone of specified pitch and duration.

Remember that the BEEP statement just makes a short attention-getting sound whose pitch and length are not under programmer control.

Amiga BASIC does not have full sound effect capability. It lacks an envelope generator that could control the attack and decay of notes. It can, however, make musical tones that are accurate in pitch.

Two, three, or four arguments are needed in the SOUND statement. The first is the pitch in cycles per second, or hertz (Hz). This variable takes values from 20 to 15000. These values span or exceed the pitch range of the human ear.

The second argument is a length number from 0 to 77. The number is the duration of the sound in terms of a clock that ticks 18.2 times a second.

Music is most conveniently made if you use the SUB programs described in Lesson 21. These make an array to hold the scale and use a string of conventional letter symbols for the melody. In this lesson, we show a simpler technique using the DATA statement to hold notes.

Questions

1. What does the statement SOUND 500,30 do?

2. Which pitch numbers give deep sounds? Which give high notes?

3. What is the largest number that you can use for making a long note?

Lesson 19. Sound

The Amiga computer has two sound statements.

BEEP   SOUND

BEEP plays one note, always the same note for the same length of time. Use it to get the user's attention.

SOUND plays a single note. You can choose both the pitch (from very low to very high) and the length of the note.

The sounds are played through the stereo jacks on the back of your computer. You can connect the *left* speaker jack to the Audio Input on the back of the monitor. Or you can connect both left and right jacks to a stereo preamplifier to play music through your stereo system.

Playing One Note
Run:

```
' Johnny One Note
' SOUND freq, duration, volume, voice
'   freq        = 20 to 15000
'   duration  = 0 to 77
'   volume    = 0 to 255
'   voice       = 0 to 3
SOUND 440,25,255,0    'concert A pitch
```

You may type just the last line in, omitting all the REMs.

(If you do not hear a sound, check that the volume is turned up on the monitor, and that a cable runs from the *left* phono jack on the back of the computer to the AUDIO INPUT jack on the monitor.)

The first number after SOUND is the pitch—low or high. Any number from 20 to 15000 is allowed, but it is easiest to hear sounds from 100 to 5000. The number is the pitch of the note measured in hertz (cycles per second).

Try this: Change the 440 pitch in "Johnny One Note" to other numbers, from 110 to 4400.

The second number is how long the note lasts—its duration. The largest number, 77, gives the longest sound—about four seconds.

The third number is how loud the sound is—its volume. The loudest is 255.

The fourth number tells which voice you want. Voices 0 and 2 play through the *left* jack; voices 1 and 3, through the *right*.

You can play simple musical tunes using SOUND statements.

Making Music

Here is a tempered scale of musical notes:

Note	Number	Note	Number
C (below middle C)	130.810	C #	277.183
C #	138.592	D	293.665
D	146.833	D #	311.127
D #	155.564	E	329.628
E	164.814	F	349.228
F	174.614	F #	369.995
F #	184.997	G	391.996
G	195.998	G #	415.305
G #	207.653	A	440.000
A	220.000	A #	466.164
A #	233.082	B	493.883
B	246.942	C (above middle C)	523.251
C (middle C)	261.626		

Playing the Scale

```
REM The Scale
FOR i=1 TO 8: READ p
SOUND p,10,255,0
NEXT i
DATA 261.626, 293.665, 329.628
DATA 349.228, 391.996, 440.000
DATA 493.883, 523.251
```

The notes of the scale of C are stored in DATA statements. Then the program reads the notes and plays them with the SOUND statement.

To make a rest in your music, use

SOUND 20,*L*,0

where *L* is the duration of the rest.

The Tempo of the Music

The second number in the SOUND statement gives the length of the note. Any number from 0 to 77 is okay. Use these numbers for a whole note in these tempos:

Largo	very slow	18
Andante	slow	15
Moderato	medium	10
Allegro	fast	8
Presto	very fast	6

Assignment 19

1. Change the "Scale" program to play in a higher octave. Just multiply all note pitches by 2 to go up by one octave.

2. Write a program to play a short tune, like "Mary Had a Little Lamb." Use a DATA statement to store the pitch numbers.

Instructor Notes 20. Drawing Pictures

In this lesson:

1. The LINE, CIRCLE, and PSET statements.
2. The x,y coordinates on the screen.
3. The line may show on the screen even if you put its ends off the screen.
4. The circle may be partly off the screen.
5. LOCATE and PRINT can put put text on the screen with the drawings.

The Amiga can produce high-resolution graphics (640 × 200 dots on the screen). In this lesson, we just make white lines on the blue screen. In a later lesson, we will extend our art work to 16 colors.

Think of the Output window as a graph with the axes crossing at the *home* position (upper left). The x-axis runs horizontally with x values from 0 to 617; y is vertical with values from 0 to 185. (Not 640 and 200 because part of the screen is window borders.) The statements PSET, LINE, and CIRCLE all use the notation (x,y) for points needed in the statement.

PSET plots a single point.

LINE needs two points, the start and the end. Lesson 23 explains how to pick a color for the line, and how to use LINE to make rectangles in outline and filled with color.

Give the center point and the radius for CIRCLE. In Lesson 23, a color is added, and you learn to draw ellipses.

BASIC does not object if part of the picture you specify is off the screen. For example, you can say CIRCLE (−20,−30),120 and only part of the circle shows on the screen. (Even the center is off the screen.)

Questions

1. Where on the screen will PSET 310,90 put a dot?

2. How do you draw a circle centered on the screen?

3. How many dots can you fit across the screen?

4. How many dots can you fit down the screen?

5. Write a short program to draw a large X on the screen.

Lesson 20. Drawing Pictures

The PSET statement lets you draw tiny dots on the screen.

The screen is like a sheet of graph paper with 617 squares across and 185 squares down.

Run:

```
REM dots
start: LOCATE 1,1
INPUT"x,y from (0,0) to (617,185)",x,y
PSET(x,y)
GOTO start
```

Try numbers near the middle and work your way to the edges. End the run with CTRL-C.

Drawing Lines

The LINE statement draws a line between two points on the screen.

Run:

```
REM bird's nest
PRINT" Give x,y of the start and the end of the line."
PRINT" x,y,x,y "
FOR t=1 TO 9000 : NEXT t : CLS
start: LOCATE 1,1
INPUT x1,y1,x2,y2
LINE (x1,y1)-(x2,y2)
FOR t=1 TO 5000 : NEXT t
LOCATE 1,1
PRINT"                                                    "
GOTO start
```

Press CRTL-C to end the run.

It is okay if the ends of the line are off the screen just so the line crosses the screen somewhere.

Drawing Circles

The CIRCLE statement draws a circle with a center point given by (x,y) and a radius r.

Run:

```
REM circles
PRINT" x, y, r "
start:
FOR t=1 TO 5000 : NEXT t
LOCATE 1,1 : PRINT"                                  "
LOCATE 1,1 : INPUT x,y,r
CIRCLE (x,y),r
LOCATE 10,20 : PRINT "circle"
GOTO start
```

It doesn't matter if the whole circle doesn't fit on the screen or even if the center of the circle is off the screen.

Mixtures of Letters and Graphics

You can mix them all up on the screen, using PRINT, PSET, LINE, and CIRCLE in the same program. Use LOCATE
to place the printing where you want
it on the screen.

Stepping Off from Here

STEP can be added to the front of an (x,y) symbol. This means you move from where you are by the distances x and y, instead of moving from the home corner by x and y.

Run:

```
REM rolling stones
PSET(20,5)
FOR i=1 TO 20
CIRCLE STEP(30,10),3+5*i
NEXT i
```

Assignment 20

1. Use CIRCLE to draw a snowperson. Use LINE for the arms, and PSET for eyes, nose, mouth, and buttons.

2. Use LINE to draw your school's initials. Save to disk.

Instructor Notes 21. Subroutines and Subprograms

In this lesson:

1. The GOSUB, RETURN, and END statements.
2. The CALL, SUB, STATIC, and END SUB statements.
3. Saving a program file in ASCII format: SAVE*"file,"*A.
4. The MERGE command.

Like GOTO, GOSUB causes a jump to another line number. But with GOSUB, control returns to the calling line when RETURN is executed.

The END statement can be put anywhere in the program, and you can use as many END statements as you wish. All that END does is to return control to the immediate mode.

Subroutines are useful in both short and long programs.

A subprogram is more flexible than a subroutine because it can be used with many different programs. Save a subprogram on disk with a special type of SAVE command:

SAVE*"filename,"*A

This format allows it to be added to the end of any other program using the MERGE command.

Call a subprogram with the CALL statement. Or call it by just using the subprogram name as the only word in a statement. (Now you see why you get an Undefined subprogram error in the Output window when you misspell a reserved word.) The computer assumes that a label will have a colon after it, while a subprogram name will not.

There are two important features of subprograms not discussed in this book: Parameters can be passed to and from a subprogram, and subprogram variables can be declared as *global* variables.

In this book, we treat only the case where subprogram variables are all local. The values of local variables apply only within the subprogram and are not carried outside the subprogram.

A subprogram's variables are declared as local by putting the word STATIC after the subprogram name. This means you can reuse the variable name in the main program or in another subprogram, and the computer does not mix them up or use the values created for one of them for any of the others.

Questions

1. What happens when the statement END is executed?

2. How is GOSUB different from GOTO?

3. What happens when RETURN is executed?

4. If RETURN is executed before GOSUB, what happens?

5. How many END statements are you allowed to put in one program?

6. Why do you want to have subroutines in your programs?
7. How are subprograms different from subroutines?

8. What does the MERGE command do? What special kind of SAVE do you use so that the subprogram can be MERGEd?

Lesson 21. Subroutines and Subprograms

Run this program, then save it to disk:

```
REM Take a trip
mainloop:
PRINT "Hop to the subroutine"
GOSUB cottage
PRINT "Back from the subroutine"
FOR T=1 TO 1000:NEXT T:PRINT
PRINT "Hop again"
GOSUB cottage
PRINT "Home for good."
END
cottage: ' subroutine
   PRINT "Got here okay."
   FOR T=1 TO 1000:NEXT T : BEEP : PRINT
   PRINT "Pack your bags, back we go."
   FOR T=1 TO 1000:NEXT T
   RETURN
```

The mainloop in this program starts in the second line and ends at END. There is a subroutine starting at cottage and ending with RETURN.

The END statement tells the computer that the program is over. The computer goes back to the immediate mode.

The GOSUB statement *calls* the subroutine. This means the computer goes and performs the instructions in the subroutine, then comes back.

The GOSUB statement is like a GOTO statement except that the computer remembers where it came from so that it can go back there again.

The RETURN statement tells the computer to go back to the statement immediately following the GOSUB.

Assignment 21A

The delay loop is written three times in the above program. Add another subroutine with a delay loop in it, and GOSUB every time you need a delay. Use the label delay.

What Good Is a Subroutine?

In a short program, a subroutine is not much good.

In a long program, it does two things:

1. It saves you work and it saves space in memory. You do not have to repeat the same program lines in different parts of the program.

2. It makes the program easier to understand and faster to write and debug.

The END Statement

The program may have zero, one, or many END statements.

Rule: The END statement tells the computer to stop running and go back to the immediate mode.

That is really all it does. You can put an END statement anywhere in the program, for example, after THEN in an IF statement.

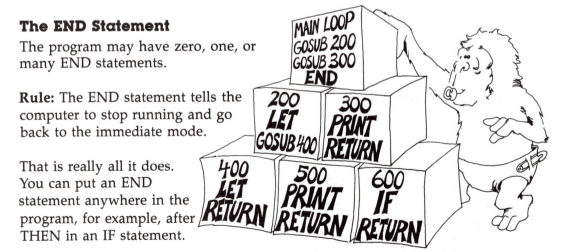

Bricks for Building Your Program

Subroutines may be called several times from different parts of the same program.

Sometimes it is better to build modules that can be used over in other programs. Then we should write them (or convert them by editing) into subprograms and save them to disk separately from the program.

Here is an example. First, we write a subprogram and save it to disk in a different way. Then we write a program that CALLs the SUBprogram.

```
SUB trademark STATIC
CLS
LOCATE 3,1
PRINT TAB(20); "Jane Ellen Smith"
PRINT TAB(20); "123 Shady Oak Street"
PRINT TAB(20); "Bad Axe MI 12345"
PRINT TAB(20); "(123) 456-7899"
PRINT
END SUB
```

The word STATIC after the subprogram name is required.

Save this subprogram to disk in ASCII format like this:

```
SAVE"trademark.sub",A
```

The .sub on the end of the name is one way of reminding yourself that this is not a program, but a subprogram.

The Master Programmer

Now write a program that needs the trademark subprogram:

```
REM Your Masterpiece
mainloop:
    ' Here starts your main loop.
    ' But first you want to identify
    ' your work to the user.
```

```
CALL trademark
   ' Now that's out of the way,
   ' let your program do its work.
END
```

Save the program like this:

```
SAVE"masterpiece"
```

Running the Combination

When it comes time to run "masterpiece", load from disk like this:

```
LOAD"masterpiece"
```

```
MERGE"trademark.sub"
```

Then RUN.

Some Shortcuts

Rather than

```
CALL trademark
```

you can omit the CALL:

```
trademark
```

If "masterpiece" always uses "trademark.sub", you can save the two together under one name. Do this:

```
LOAD"masterpiece"
```

```
MERGE"trademark.sub"
```

```
SAVE"masterpiece.full"
```

You do not need the ,A on the SAVE when doing this because you will not use the MERGE statement when loading.

Assignment 21B

1. Write a short program that uses subroutines. It doesn't have to do anything useful, just print some silly things.

   In it put three subroutines:

   Call one of them twice from the main program.
   Call one of them from another subroutine.
   Call one of them from an IF statement.

2. Write a short subprogram and save it with SAVE"*filename*",A. Then write a short program that calls the subprogram. MERGE the subprogram into the program and save them both. Run the combination.

Instructor Notes 22. Windows and Color

In this lesson:

1. The SCREEN statement.
2. The WINDOW statement.
3. The COLOR and the PALETTE statements revisited.
4. A SUBprogram for mixing colors.

The SCREEN statement reserves room in memory for a window. The standard BASIC Output window uses a high-resolution, noninterlaced screen with four colors. If you want more than four colors, you need to use SCREEN to reserve more memory. We will use only one set of options: high-resolution, noninterlaced, full-size screen with 16 colors. This option is not standard in BASIC because it uses four times as much memory as the 4-color screen.

The WINDOW statement actually opens the window for view. There are many options available, including small windows, the use of the mouse to move and re-size the window, and so forth. But we will discuss only the full-size window because that gives most room for drawing.

Questions

1. Suppose your program has the statement SCREEN 3,640,200,4,2. What does this do?

2. Now add to your program to open a window with the name "Drawing Pad"? How do you do this?

3. How many colors are there to choose from?

Lesson 22. Windows and Color

In Lesson 20, we made white drawings on a blue background. Now let's put 16 different colors on the screen at once.

The SCREEN statement is used to set aside some memory for a 16-color window. Then the WINDOW statement displays a new Output window to paint on.

SCREEN   2,   640,   200,   4,   2

            id,   width,   height,   depth,   mode

(id = identification number)

We will always use the same SCREEN numbers you see here. It saves enough memory for a full-size, high-resolution screen with 16 colors. (The depth number helps tell how many colors you can put on the screen. Mode 2 is for high-resolution, no line interlacing.)

Depth Number	Number of Colors
1	2
2	4
3	8
4	16
5	32

(Depth 5 cannot be used with mode 2 or 4.)

The WINDOW Statement
WINDOW 2,"Hot Stuff", , ,2

WINDOW *id,"window title", , ,screen id number*

The *id* for the usual Output window in BASIC is 1. So you can use number 2, 3, or 4 (or 1 if you don't mind messing up the standard Output window).

If you want your window to appear on the screen you have created, you must execute a SCREEN statement before your WINDOW statement. The screen id number in the WINDOW statement must be the same as the id number in the SCREEN statement.

The *"window title"* is a string constant that appears in the title bar of the window.

```
REM An open and shut window
SCREEN 3, 640, 200, 4, 2
WINDOW 4,"Hot Stuff",,,3
WINDOW CLOSE 4
SCREEN CLOSE 3
END
```

Assignment 22A

Add to the above program so that it prints **Here we are!** when the window Hot Stuff is open. Let it print **Back again** when you have returned to the standard BASIC Output window.

Sixteen Colors

Now that we have saved room for 16 colors in the screen memory, how do we put the colors on the screen? Use the COLOR statement you learned about in Lesson 4, but now with colors from 0 through 15 in the *text* and the *background* places.

COLOR *text,background*

Jumping Rainbow Sentence

Run:

```
REM jumping rainbow sentence
RANDOMIZE TIMER
SCREEN 3,640,200,4,2
WINDOW 5,,,,3
COLOR 2,2 : CLS            ' clear background to black
FOR I=1 TO 9              ' read 9 words
READ w$
x=FIX(RND*55)+1          ' which column
y=FIX(RND*19)+1          ' which row
c=FIX(RND*11)+4          ' which color
COLOR c,2                ' set text color
LOCATE y,x : PRINT w$    ' place the cursor
FOR t=1 TO 1000 : NEXT t
NEXT I
FOR t=1 TO 4000 : NEXT t
WINDOW CLOSE 5
SCREEN CLOSE 3
DATA Watch, out, your, pop, is
DATA spilling, on, your, keyboard.
```

Rainbow Ball

```
REM rainbow ball
SCREEN 3,640,200,4,2
WINDOW 3,,,,3
C=3 : COLOR c,2 : CLS
FOR I=1 TO 60
1 LOCATE 12,I
2 PRINT "O"
3 FOR T=1 TO 200 : NEXT T
4 LOCATE 12,I:PRINT " ";
5 C=C+1 : IF C>15 THEN C=3
6 COLOR C,2
NEXT I
WINDOW CLOSE 3
SCREEN CLOSE 3
COLOR 1,0
```

The FOR-NEXT loop moves a ball across the screen, changing its color as it goes.

Lines 1 and 2 put the ball on the screen in a new spot.

Then line 3 waits for a moment.

Line 4 erases the ball that was just printed.

Line 5 increases the color number by one each time the ball is moved. When the color number reaches 16, it changes back to color 3.

Assignment 22B

1. Change the rainbow ball so that it falls instead of moving across the screen.

2. Add to the number guessing game in Lesson 12 so that a large colored star shows when the correct answer is guessed. Use a timing loop so that the star shows for a few seconds before the game starts again.

3. Write a program to draw Sinbad's Magic Carpet. Let the user choose how many colors are in the rug, and what colors. Then draw a pattern of colored letters on the screen.

4. Make a program to write your name in a big colored X on the screen.

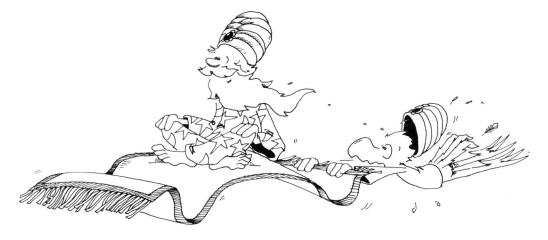

Instructor Notes 23.   Color Graphics

In this lesson:

1. Line drawings in the colors of your choice: PSET, LINE, CIRCLE.
2. The LINE statement with B for "draw a box" and F for "fill with color."
3. The PAINT statement for filling areas with color.
4. Arcs of circles with CIRCLE.
5. Angles are given in radians.
6. Making "pies" by using negative angles in CIRCLE.
7. Making ellipses by changing the "shape" number.

This lesson tells how to draw and paint in 16 colors (high-resolution graphics).

Amiga BASIC uses a *palette*, with 16 numbered positions (0–15) on which to place colors that you mix yourself from the primary colors red, yellow, and blue.

The colors can be used in printing and in graphics. In printing, the COLOR statement specifies the text and the background colors.

In graphics, the background is selected with a COLOR statement, but the colors of the lines and solids are specified in the PSET, LINE, and CIRCLE statements at the time of drawing.

Any closed area can be filled with solid color by the PAINT statement. The point (x,y) must be inside the area to be colored. The color number tells which paint dab defined by a PALETTE statement to paint with.

The border number in the PAINT statement tells the color of the border of the area being filled in with color. If a border color is not specified, then it is the same as the fill color.

The LINE statement also allows you to draw rectangular boxes. Just add the letter *B* (for box) on the end of the statement. Adding *BF* (for box fill) makes the box a solid color.

Arcs of circles require adding two angles to the CIRCLE statement: the beginning and ending angles of the arc. These angles are measured in radians, and this is explained in the lesson. If an angle is negative, then a line connects its end of the arc to the center of the circle. If both angles are negative, you can make sections for pie charts.

Finally, the "circle" can have unequal radii, making it an ellipse, or the arc of an ellipse.

Questions

1. How do you make a rectangle with upper left corner at (30,10) and lower right corner at (60,110)?

2. How many palettes can you choose from? What colors are on each one?

3. What does the (30,40) mean in this statement:

   PAINT (30,40),3,1

   What does the 3 mean?
   What does the 1 mean?

4. What does the 2 mean in

   CIRCLE (90,112),55,2

5. How would you paint the above circle a solid white? (Your answer should say something about PALETTE and something about PAINT.

Lesson 23. Color Graphics

To draw dots, lines, and circles in the colors of your choice, add a color number to PSET, LINES, and CIRCLE.

Example:

```
REM colored lines
PALETTE 3,.7,.2,.2
PSET(160,100),3
LINE(20,20)–(400,150),3
CIRCLE(160,100),50,3
```

The color number in the PSET, LINE, or CIRCLE statement tells what color on the palette you will paint with.

```
PSET ( x, y),color
LINE (x1,y1)–(x2,y2),color
CIRCLE ( x, y),radius, color
```

Outline a Colored Box

The LINE statement can also draw a rectangle. Just add the letter *B* (for *box*) after the color number.

Run:

```
LINE (60,80)–(120,160),3
LINE (50,70)–(130,170),3,B
```

Solid Color for the Box

By adding an *F*, you'll change the outline box into a solid color box.

```
LINE (50,70)–(130,170),3,BF
```

The letter *F* stands for *fill* and means the computer fills in the box outline with color.

Solid Colors for Everything

The PAINT statement fills in any shape outline with color. Make the outline by drawing lines with LINE or circles with CIRCLE.

Try:

```
REM Hard Ball
CIRCLE (300,100),80,1
PAINT (300,100),1
```

The (x,y) point in the PAINT must be inside the circle. But it doesn't matter where. Try changing the value in the above PAINT statement to (379,100) and run it again. It still works. But try (381,100), and it colors the whole screen outside the circle.

Dueling Artists

Here is a program that fills both circles and rectangles with solid colors.

Run:

```
REM dueling artists
SCREEN 2,640,200,4,2
WINDOW 2,,,,2
COLOR 0,2:CLS
```

```
FOR b=3 TO 13
CIRCLE (200,90),150,b
PAINT (150,90),b
FOR t=1 to 500:NEXT t
LINE (270,20)-(600,160),b+2,bf
NEXT b
FOR t=1 to 5000:NEXT t
SCREEN CLOSE 2
WINDOW CLOSE 2
COLOR 1,0
```

Pies, Bananas, and Pancakes

The CIRCLE statement makes arcs of circles, and also ellipses and arcs of ellipses. (An ellipse is a squashed circle.)

CIRCLE *(x,y),radius,color,start angle,end angle,shape*

There are three tricks here. The first is in the angles. They are measured in radians, not degrees.

Degrees	Radians	
360	2*pi	Full circle
180	pi	Half circle
90	pi/2	Right angle

And so forth. Pi is, of course, our old friend 3.1416.

The second trick is in making real pies rather than arcs. You just make the two angles negative. Then a straight line connects the center of the circle with each end of the arc. You have a "pie."

The third trick is in the shape. If *shape* = 0.44, then you get a circle. If *shape* is smaller, the "circle" looks squashed, as if you sat on a soft basketball. If *shape* is larger than 0.44, the "circle" looks like a football standing on end.

CIRCLE (300,100),60,3,0,3.14	Makes a half circle, color 3
CIRCLE (300,100),60,3,−.1,−.5	Makes a piece of pie
CIRCLE (300,100),60,3,,,.1	Makes a squashed ball
CIRCLE (300,100),60,3,,,3	Makes a football on end

Try:

```
REM bananas
RANDOMIZE TIMER
SCREEN 2,640,200,4,2
WINDOW 2,,,,2
COLOR 0,2:CLS
pi=3.14159265#
FOR i=1 TO 100
x=FIX(RND*600)
y=FIX(RND*180)
r=FIX(RND*100)+10
c=FIX(RND*16)
a=FIX(RND*2*pi)
b=FIX(RND*2*pi)
q=RND*1+.1
CIRCLE(x,y),r,c,a,b,q
NEXT i
FOR t=1 to 3000:NEXT t
WINDOW CLOSE 2
SCREEN CLOSE 2
COLOR 1,0
```

Assignment 23

1. Draw your school's initials, and make them
   flash on and off with your school's colors.

2. Draw the flag of your country and color
   it correctly.

153

Instructor Notes 24. Arrays and the DIM Statement

In this lesson:

1. The DIM statement.
2. Arrays as families with members.
3. The array name is the family name.
4. Members have first names in parentheses. These are the indices, or subscripts.
5. Each member is stored in its own box.
6. Array members have numeric or string values.
7. Each array member has a value of zero, or empty, for numbers and strings, respectively, before its first use.

Arrays with one index are described first. The array itself is compared to a family, and the individual elements of the array to family members. The index value is the "first name" of the member.

Two-dimensional arrays can be compared to the numbers on a calendar month page or the rectangular array of cells on the TV screen.

The concept of arrays is not too difficult. The trick is to see how they help in programming. There are a large variety of uses for arrays, and many do not seem to fall into recognizable categories.

You can use them to store lists of information. Connected lists also can occur. The telephone number program uses two-line arrays—one for names, the other for numbers. They are indexed the same, so a single index number can retrieve both the name and the number that goes with it.

Another general use of arrays is to store numbers which cannot neatly be obtained from an equation. An example is the number of days in each of the 12 months.

Games often use two-dimensional arrays or greater to store information about the playing board.

If you forget to DIMension an array before use, the BASIC interpreter gives it a dimension of 10. If you try to use an element larger than that assigned to the array, the Subscript out of range error message is printed.

Questions

1. What does the DIM BD(6) statement do?

2. Where do you put the DIM statement in the program?

3. What is the index, or subscript, of an array?

Lesson 24. Arrays and the DIM Statement

Meet the Array family. Each member of the family is a variable. The f$ family are string variables.

f$(0)="dad"
f$(1)="mom"
f$(2)="Karen"

Here is a family of numeric variables:

N(0)= 43
N(1)= 13
N(2)= 0
N(3)= 0

The family has a "last name" like A( ) or B$( ). Each member has a number inside the ( ) for a "first name." The array always starts with the first name 0.

Instead of family, we should say *array*.

Instead of first name, we should say *index number*, or *subscript*.

The DIM Statement Reserves Boxes

When the Array family go to a movie, they always reserve seats first. They use a DIM statement to do this.

The DIM statement tells the computer to reserve a row of boxes for the array. DIM stands for DIMension which means size.

DIM A(3)

saves four memory boxes, one each for the variables A(0), A(1), A(2), and A(3). These boxes are for numbers and contain the number 0 to start with. Another example:

DIM A(3),b$(4)

This time, DIM reserves four boxes for the A( ) array and five for the string array b$( ). The boxes named b$(0) through b$(4) are for strings and are empty to start with.

Rule: Put the DIM statement early in the program, before the array is used in any other statement.

Making a List

Enter:

```
REM In a row
DIM A$(5)
PRINT" Enter a word:"
FOR N=0 TO 5
INPUT A$(N) : PRINT
IF N<>5 THEN PRINT"Another:"
NEXT N : PRINT
REM Put in a row
PRINT" Here they are in a row:"
PRINT : PRINT" ";
FOR I=0 TO 5
PRINT A$(I);" ";
NEXT I
```

You can use a member of the array by itself. Look at this line:

Boat$(2)="yellow submarine"

Or the array can be used in a loop where the index keeps changing. Find two places in the program "In a row" that do this.

Making Two Lists
Enter:

```
REM Phone List
DIM Nam$(20), Num$(20) 'NAME is a reserved word
PRINT " Enter names and numbers:"
PRINT " (Enter 'Q' to quit)" : PRINT
I=0
enter:
INPUT " Name:      ",Nam$(I)
IF UCASE$(Nam$(I))="Q" THEN tail
INPUT " Number:   ",Num$(I) : PRINT
```

```
I=I+1 : GOTO enter
tail:
PRINT
FOR Z=1 TO I-1
PRINT Nam$(Z);TAB(20);Num$(Z)
NEXT Z
```

One Dimension, Two Dimension,...

The arrays that have one index are called one-dimensional arrays.

But arrays can have two or more indices. Two-dimensional arrays have their family members put in a rectangle like the days in a month on a calendar.

The DIM statement for a two-dimensional array has two numbers in it. For example,

```
DIM stuff(2,3)
stuff(0,1)=3.14159265
```

The Magic Square

Use the Edit menu features Cut, Copy, and Paste to help enter this program. Copy the row starting s(1,1) and then paste it twice below itself. Then edit these two rows with the BACK SPACE and number keys.

Likewise, the FOR loops can be copied and edited.

Run:

```
REM Magic Square
setup:
    s(1,1)=8 : s(1,2)=3 : s(1,3)=4
    s(2,1)=1 : s(2,2)=5 : s(2,3)=9
    s(3,1)=6 : s(3,2)=7 : s(3,3)=2
PRINT " The magic square:"
    FOR j=1 TO 3 : PRINT TAB(20);
    FOR i=1 TO 3 : PRINT s(j,i);
    NEXT i,j
done:
    PRINT
    PRINT " The sums:"
    FOR j=1 to 3: t=0
    FOR i=1 to 3: t=t+s(j,i)
    NEXT i
    PRINT " Row";j;"sums to    ";t
    NEXTj
```

Assignment 24

1. Write a program that stores the number of days in each month in an array. Then when you ask the user to enter a number <1 to 12>, it prints out the number of days in that month. Use a DATA statement to hold the days. Then READ the data into the array by using a loop.

2. Write a program so that the computer plays the card game War against the user. Have an array hold the 52 cards in the deck. Deal them at random into two arrays, one for each player. In each turn of play, each player plays the cards from his or her deck in order. If the cards played by user and computer

160

don't match, they both are put in the booty pile. If they do match, there will be a battle. In the battle, both players play their next cards. The high card wins the whole booty pile.

3. Add to the "Magic Square" program so that the sum of each column and the sum of each of the two diagonals of the square are printed out.

Instructor Notes 25. Snipping Strings: LEFT$, MID$, RIGHT$, LEN

In this lesson:

1. The functions LEFT$, MID$, RIGHT$, LEN.
2. Concatenation.
3. LEN counts all characters, even spaces.
4. The < symbol can test strings for alphabetical order.
5. The INSTR( ) function.

These functions together with the concatenation operation (+) allow complete freedom to cut up strings and glue them back in any order.

The MID$ function in Amiga BASIC exists in three forms. The only form discussed in this book is the one with three arguments. The second form, with the last argument omitted, is similar to the RIGHT$ function. A third form allows a part of one string to be substituted for another. While this may be handy at times, its syntax is unlike any other BASIC function. When a student is more experienced in using string functions, reading the Amiga BASIC manual plus some experimenting should suffice to learn the extended forms of the MID$ function.

The LEN function counts the characters in a string, including punctuation and spaces. Counting spaces may confuse the student.

The less-than (<) and greater-than (>) signs in an IF statement may be used to test which of two strings comes first alphabetically. If the first letters of the two strings are identical, then the second letters are tested automatically. Very handy. However, the ASCII number is being tested, so A and a are not the same in this test. The UCASE$ function can be used to put all letter characters into capitals before the test is done.

The INSTR function is perfect when you need to search for a small string buried in a longer string.

Questions

1. If you want to save the STAR from STARS AND STRIPES, what function will you use? What arguments?

2. If you want to count the number of characters in the string PQ$, what function do you use? What argument?

3. What is wrong with each of these lines?

   A$=LEFT$(4,D$)
   RIGHT$(R$,3)="pqrst"
   F$=MID$(A,3)
   J$=LEFT(R$,YT)

4. What two arguments does the RIGHT$( ) function need?

5. What function will snip the third and fourth letters out of a word.

6. Write a short program that takes the word *computer* and makes it into *putercom.*

Lesson 25. Snipping Strings: LEFT$, MID$, RIGHT$, LEN

Gluing Strings

You already know how to glue strings together:

a$="con" + "cat" + "en" + "ation"
PRINT a$

The real name for gluing is *concatenation*.

Concatenation means "make a chain." Maybe we should call them chains instead of strings.

Snipping Strings

Let's cut a piece off a string. Enter and run:

REM Snipping the left end off
PRINT" Changing Spanish to French"
s$="Amiga"
PRINT" The Spanish say ";s$
f$=LEFT$(s$,3)
PRINT" The French say ";f$

The LEFT$ function snips off the left end of the string. The snipped off piece can be put into a string variable box or printed or whatever.

Rule: The LEFT$( ) function needs two things inside the parentheses:

1. The string you want to snip.
2. The number of characters you want to keep.

Snipping the Other End

RIGHT$( ) is like LEFT$( ), except the characters are saved off the right end of the string. The order of the letters is still left to right.

More Snipping and Gluing

Run:

```
REM Scissors and Glue
shelly$="clambake"
PRINT" What do you do at a ";shelly$+"?"
PRINT" You ";
PRINT RIGHT$(shelly$,4)+"   "+LEFT$(shelly$,4)+"s."
```

The pieces of string you snip off can be glued back together in a different order.

How Long Is the String?

Run:

```
REM Long rope
INPUT " Give me a word: ",word$
PRINT
l=LEN(word$)
PRINT " The string: '";word$;"' "
PRINT " is ";l;"characters long."
```

The function LEN( ) tells the number of characters in the string. It counts everything in the string, even the spaces.

Cutting a Piece Out of the Middle

The MID$ function cuts a piece out of the middle of the string.

Run:

```
REM Sailor
PRINT" How do you row a boat?"
plank$="board"
PRINT" Take a ";plank$;
twig$=MID$(plank$,2,3)
PRINT" and cut off the part that is an";twig$;"."
```

The line twig$=MID$(plank$,2,3) means:

Get the string from box plank$ (this box holds *board*). Count over two letters and start saving letters into box twig$. Save three letters. They are *oar*.

Look Ma, No Spaces

Enter:

```
REM no spaces
PRINT:PRINT
PRINT "Give me a long sentence"
PRINT
INPUT S$
L=LEN(S$)
T$=" "
FOR I=1 TO L
L$=MID$(S$,I,1)
IF L$<>" " THEN T$=T$+L$
NEXT I
PRINT:PRINT T$
```

Line L$=MID$(S$,I,1) snips just one letter at a time from the middle of the string.

Alphabetical Order

Try these:

```
IF "A" < "B" THEN PRINT "A comes before B"
IF "ca"<"cz" THEN PRINT "CA comes before CZ"
```

Run each one. Then change the < to a > and run again. The less-than and greater-than signs can be used to see if two strings are in alphabetical order.

A String Within a String

The INSTR function tells how far into a long string a short piece of string is buried.

Run:

```
REM dig me out
m$ = "ldoubodjcugmldkijrockbloyubfundywkkfdbdylkdofgkodyvnsbod
      majru"
PRINT" Where is the fun in all this?"
x = INSTR(m$,"fun")
PRINT" X marks the spot: ";x
```

Count along in m$ and see that the number x is the location of the letter f in *fun*.

Assignment 25

1. Write a secret cipher making program. You give it a sentence, and it finds how long the sentence is. Then it switches the first letter with the second, the third with the fourth, and so on. Example:

   THIS IS A TEST   becomes   HTSII S AETTS

2. Write a question answering program. You give it a question starting with a verb, and it reverses verb and noun to answer the question. Example:

   ARE YOU A TURKEY?   becomes   YOU ARE A TURKEY.

3. Write a Pig Latin program. It asks for a word. Then it takes all the letters up to the first vowel and puts them on the back of the word, followed by *AY*. If the word starts with a vowel, it adds only *LAY*. Examples:

   BOX   becomes   OXBAY
   APPLE   becomes   APPLELAY

Instructor Notes 26. Music

In this lesson:

1. Subprogram for defining the chromatic tempered scale.
2. A music notation both the user and the computer can understand.
3. Subprogram to play a single note, given the notation for it.
4. Main program to play "Row, Row, Row."

The SOUND statement plays a note of a given pitch and duration. To make music, the pitch must belong to a scale, and the durations must allow music in good tempo. By creating a subprogram, "note", to do all the work, we'll be able to use the subprogram in any other future music-making programs.

The tempered scale is defined as 12 notes that divide an octave into equal intervals. By "equal intervals" we do *not* mean equally spaced in frequency, but rather that each note is higher in frequency than the previous one by the same factor.

The pitch, frequency in cycles per second, increases by a factor of two for the same note in the next higher octave. So we need a number that multiplied by itself 12 times gives 2. This is a job for the exponential and logarithmic functions, but they are not explained in this book.

The computer now is in tune and knows how to make notes of various lengths. It is time to pick a notation to replace the staff notation read by musicians. Our notation should be easy to type, easy to remember, and easy to form as we read the staff notation.

We store our music in DATA statements, and each note occupies four characters. The first two are the letter name of the note, with a space or a # sign after it as appropriate. The second two letters tell the note length. For example QQ for a quarter note and Q. for a dotted quarter note. (The doubling of the Q has no meaning, but a second Q makes for easier reading than just putting a space there.)

Having settled the notation, we write the music subprogram to read a four-character note and convert it to the two numbers, pitch and duration, needed by the SOUND statement. It then sounds the note and returns to the main program which gives it the next note.

All this is a bit complicated and may be too difficult for younger children. If you find your student becoming frustrated with this material, you may want to skip this lesson.

Although the concepts here are complex, once mastered, your student will be able to add music to any program with a minimum of fuss. The Amiga runs so fast that it has time to do all this music notation translating and still be able to do other things while the music is playing.

Questions

1. How do subprograms help save us work?

2. What does a dot after a note mean?

3. What does C# mean in a our string of music?

4. What does + mean in our string?

5. How do you tell the computer to play a half note?

Lesson 26.   Music

A music-playing subprogram is an excellent example of the advantage of using
subprograms.

First, we write a subprogram to tell the computer how to play in tune and to keep
good tempo. We will call it "notes".

Then we write a subprogram to play just one note, for example, "play a quarter
note in C#." We will call this subprogram "music".

Finally, we write a main program that plays some tune. We will play "Row, Row,
Row."

The subprograms "notes" and "music" can be used over and over again, whenever you want to have some music in one of your programs. Just MERGE them
onto the end of whatever program needs music.

The Notes Subprogram

Enter:

```
SUB notes(ca,a(1),t(1)) STATIC
  ' defines a tempered scale at the lowest octave
  ' stores note durations
  f=EXP(LOG(2)/12)
  n=ca/8          ' ca is "concert a" or about 445 Hz.
  FOR i=1 TO 12
    a(i)=n        ' a(i) is an array of 12 notes in an octave
    n=n*f         ' f is the twelth root of 2
  NEXT i
  t=1
  FOR i=1 TO 12 STEP 2
    t(i)=t : t(i+1)=t*1.5
    t=t*2
  NEXT i
END SUB
```

Save to disk:

SAVE"notes.sub",A

171

This subprogram uses two arrays: a(i) holds the pitch numbers of the 12 notes of an octave, and t(i) holds the note length numbers from a dotted whole note to a sixteenth note.

First, the subprogram picks the pitch for concert A. The frequency of this note is about 445 hertz (Hz). You can change the number 445 a little to bring the computer in tune with any instruments you want to play along with the computer.

Then the pitches of the 12 notes are made by a mathematical trick. You do not need to understand how the EXP and LOG functions do this. The pitches are stored in the array a(i).

Finally, the set of note lengths are made and stored in t(i).

Writing Music Without a Staff

Musicians use a musical staff to write the notes. We need to choose some other way to tell the computer which note to play. It should be easy to look at a staff of notes and then write the correct translation for the computer to use.

Here is how the first two measures of "Row, Row, Row" will look. There are five notes:

DATA C Q., C Q., C QQ, D II, E Q.

In words, the pitches are C, C, C, D, E.

In words, the lengths are dotted quarter, dotted quarter, quarter, eighth, dotted quarter. (Remember that a dot after a quarter note means "hold it as long as a quarter and an eighth together.")

So each note takes exactly four spaces in the DATA statement—the first two for the note pitch, and the second two for the note length.

Note names:

A   A#   B   C   C#   D   D#   E   F   F#   G   G#

Note lengths:

W.   dotted whole (worth 1½ whole notes)
WW   whole
H.   dotted half
HH   half
Q.   dotted quarter
QQ   quarter
I.   dotted eighth (we don't want to call it E!)
II   eighth
S.   dotted sixteenth
SS   sixteenth

The Music Subprogram

Enter:

```
SUB music( s$,b(1),t(),m) STATIC
  l$ =" A A#B C C#D D#E F F#G G#" 'find the pitch
   n$=LEFT$( s$,2)
   n =INSTR(l$,n$)/2
   f =b(n)*8*m
  d$ =" SSS.III.QQQ.HHH.WWW."        'find the duration
   t$=RIGHT$(s$,2)
   i =INSTR(d$,t$)/2
   t =t(i)*2
  SOUND f,t : SOUND 50,1            'play the note and stop it
END SUB
```

173

Save to disk with this format:

SAVE"music.sub",A

This subprogram starts by putting names of the 12 notes in the string l$. Only sharps are used in these names—no flats. You could modify the program so that flats come in, too.

Next, the note string from the Row, Row, Row program is broken into its two parts—the first two letters being the note name and the second giving the note duration.

Then the computer searches l$ to find the note name. It counts how far into l$ the note is because this tells how far into the array b(i) its pitch number is.

In the same manner, the note duration (like QQ) is located in d$, and this tells where in t(i) the duration number is. These two numbers are put into the SOUND statement, and the note comes out. Then the "music" subprogram sends the computer back to the main program.

Merging Programs

Below is the Row, Row, Row program. The program is in three parts. The second and third parts are the two subprograms from above: "music" and "notes". You do not need to retype these parts. The whole purpose of subprograms is that you can reuse them in other programs.

To enter Row, Row, Row, begin by entering **NEW**, and enter only the first part of the program up to and including the END statement. Next, activate the Output window by clicking in it and enter

MERGE "music.sub"

You will notice that "music.sub" has been added (appended) to the end of the program in memory, Row, Row, Row. To append the final part of our program, enter this in the Output window:

MERGE "notes.sub"

Here's a copy of all three parts put together. Remember, you do not have to re-type the last two parts:

```
REM Row, row, row
    DIM b(13),t(13)            'holds 12 notes in an octave
    ca=445 : m=1               'is "concert A" pitch
    CALL notes(ca,b(),t())     'stores the frequencies & durations
    RESTORE song
getnote:
    READ s$                    'get the note
    IF s$="+" THEN m=m*2 : GOTO getnote
    IF s$="-" THEN m=m/2 : GOTO getnote
    IF s$="END" THEN END       'note: END must be capital letters
    CALL music(s$,b(),t(),m) 'SOUND plays the note
GOTO getnote
song:
    DATA C Q.,C Q.,C QQ,D II,E Q.
    DATA E QQ,D II,E QQ,F II,G H.,+    ,
    DATA C II,C II,C II,-    ,G II,G II,G II
    DATA E II,E II,E II,C II,C II,C II
    DATA G QQ,F II,E QQ,D II,C H.,END
END
```

```
SUB music( s$,b(1),t(),m) STATIC
  l$ =" A A#B C C#D D#E F F#G G#"  'find the pitch
   n$=LEFT$( s$,2)
   n =INSTR(l$,n$)/2
   f =b(n)*8*m
  d$ =" SSS.III.QQQ.HHH.WWW."        'find the duration
   t$=RIGHT$(s$,2)
   i =INSTR(d$,t$)/2
   t =t(i)*2
  SOUND f,t : SOUND 5Ø,1             'play the note and stop it
END SUB

SUB notes(ca,a(1),t(1)) STATIC
  ' defines a tempered scale at the lowest octave
  ' stores note durations
  f=EXP(LOG(2)/12)
  n=ca/8              ' ca is "concert a" or about 445 Hz.
  FOR i=1 TO 12
     a(i)=n           ' a(i) is an array of 12 notes in an octave
     n=n*f            ' f is the twelfth root of 2
  NEXT i
  t=1
  FOR i=1 TO 12 STEP 2
    t(i)=t : t(i+1)=t*1.5
    t=t*2
  NEXT i
END SUB
```

The first part of the program calls the
"notes" subprogram to make the arrays.
Then starting at the getnote label, the
program reads the DATA statements one
note at a time and calls the "music" subprogram
to play each note. The last note is not a note at all,
but the word END. The computer knows the tune is over.

Writing Other Tunes

To change music from "staff" to "computer" notation, read the notes on the staff, and write them on paper like this: *name, length*. When you come to a bar mark in the score, write a bar mark on the paper.

Now put the notes from the paper into DATA statements. It is easier to check the program against the paper if each DATA statement holds one or two full bars. The start of Row Row, Row looks like this:

DATA C Q., C Q., C QQ, D II, E Q.

One other thing goes into the DATA statement. If you want the notes to play an octave higher, you put a plus sign (+) followed by three spaces. If you want to play an octave lower, use a minus sign (−).

Assignment 26

1. Change the string in the Row, Row, Row program so that it plays very fast, very slow, an octave higher, an octave lower.

2. Change the Row, Row, Row program so that it plays another tune.

Instructor Notes 27.   Switching Numbers with Strings

In this lesson:

1. The STR$ and the VAL functions.
2. Review of functions and their arguments.
3. Functions compared with statements.
4. Meaning of *return a value.*
5. Arguments which are functions.

STR$ takes an argument that is a number and changes it into a string that has the same appearance.

VAL takes a string and creates a numeric value from it. It accepts decimals and scientific notation (such as $1.2E+13$). If the first character is not a decimal digit, or a plus or minus sign, it returns the value zero. Otherwise, it scans the number, terminating at the first nonnumeric character (other than the E of the scientific notation).

This interconversion of the two main types of variables—numeric and string— adds great flexibility to programs involving numbers.

You can slice up a number and rearrange its digits by first converting it to a string. This is demonstrated in the "numbers into strings" example. The assigned problem that makes a number play leapfrog by repeatedly putting its rear digit in the front uses this idea.

Questions

1. If your number "marches" too quickly in your solution to assignmant 27-2, how do you slow it down?

2. If your program has the string "GEORGE WASHINGTON WAS BORN IN 1732," write a few lines to answer the question "How long ago was Washington born?" (You need to get the birth date out of the string and convert it to a number.)

3. What is a "value." What is meant by "a function returns a value"? What are some of the things you can do with the value?

4. What is an argument of a function? How many arguments does the RIGHT$( ) function have? How many for the CHR$( ) function?

5. Each line below has errors. Explain what is wrong.

```
FIX(Q)=65
D$=LEFT(R$,1)
PW$=VAL(F$)
PRINT CHR$
```

Lesson 27. Switching Numbers with Strings

This lesson explains two functions: VAL( ) and STR$( ).

Making Strings into Numbers

We have two kinds of variables—strings and numbers. We can change one kind into the other.

Run:

```
REM Making strings into numbers
L$ = "123" : M$ = "789"
L = VAL(L$) : M = VAL(M$)
PRINT L : PRINT M : PRINT " ---"
PRINT L+M
```

VAL stands for *value*. It changes the string into a number, if it can.

180

Making Numbers into Strings

Run:

```
REM Making numbers into strings
PRINT
INPUT " Give me a number ",NB
PRINT
N$=STR$(NB) : L=LEN(N$)
FOR I=L TO 1 STEP −1
B$=B$+MID$(N$,I,1)
NEXT I
PRINT " Here it is backward ";B$
```

STR$ stands for *string*. It changes a number into a string.

Functions Again

In this book we use these functions:

RND( )   FIX( )
LEFT$( )   RIGHT$( )
MID$( )   LEN( )
VAL( )   STR$( )
ASC( )   CHR$( )
UCASE$( )

Rules About Functions

Functions may have ( ) with one or more arguments inside them. For example,

MID$(D$,5,J) has three arguments: D$, 5, and J.

The arguments may be numbers or strings or both.

A function is not a statement. It cannot begin a line.

Right: D=LEN$(CS$)

Wrong: LEN (CS$)=5

A function acts just like a number or a string. We say the function returns a value. The value can be put in a box or printed just like any other number or string. The function may even be an argument in another function.

The arguments tell which value is returned.

(Remember, string values go in string variable boxes; numeric values go in numeric boxes.)

Practice with Functions

For each function in the list below, give the name of the agrument, and tell whether the argument value is a number or a string. Tell whether the argument is a variable, constant, or function.

FIX(Q)   fn   _____

                  arg   _____

MID$(RI$,E,2)   fn   _____

                  arg   _____

                  arg   _____

                  arg   _____

VAL(ER$)   fn   _____

                  arg   _____

STR$(RND*91)   fn   _____

                  arg   _____

Assignment 27

1. Write a program that asks the user for a number. Then make another number that is backward from the first, and add them together. Print all three numbers like an addition problem (with plus sign and a line under the numbers).

2. Make a number "leapfrog" slowly across the screen. First, write it on the screen. Then take its left digit and move it to the front. Keep repeating. Don't forget to erase each digit when you move it.

Instructor Notes 28. ASCII Code, ON-GOTO

In this lesson:

1. ASCII numbers explained.
2. The ASC( ) and CHR$( ) functions.
3. ASCII extended to foreign letters.
4. The SWAP function.
5. The MOUSE statement.
6. The ON-GOTO and ON-GOSUB statements.

This lesson treats the ASCII code for characters and the functions ASC( ) and CHR$( ) that change characters into ASCII numbers and vice versa.

The ASCII code is primarily intended to standardize signals between hardware pieces such as computers with printers, terminals, and other computers. But within programs the ASCII numbers also are useful. The letters are numbered in increasing order, so the ASCII numbers are useful in alphabetizing. The numeric digits are also in order, and the punctuation marks have ASCII numbers.

Strictly speaking, there are only 128 ASCII characters, and some of these are supposed to signal mechanical actions on a Teletype machine. It is more convenient to define a full byte's worth of characters (making 256 characters), and each computer manufacturer uses the extra characters in a unique way. Commodore assigns them to various graphics, math, and foreign language symbols.

The SWAP statement takes any two variables (numeric or string) and exchanges their values.

A "sketcher" program demonstrates the MOUSE statement and reviews other elements of good program design.

The ON-GOTO and ON-GOSUB statements allow a variable that takes on consecutive values 1, 2, 3, 4,..., to send control to various places in the program.

Questions

1. Does ASC(*S*$) return a string or a number for its value?

2. Does ASC(*S*$) have a string or a number for its argument?

3. Same two questions for CHR$(*N*).

4. Which letter has the larger ASCII code number, *B* or *W*?

5. Do you know the ASCII number for the character 1? Is it the number 1?

6. What will the computer do if you run this line:

   PRINT CHR$(32); CHR$(65)

   Try it.

Lesson 28. ASCII Code, ON-GOTO

Numbering the Letters in the Alphabet

That's easy, you say. "A is 1, B is 2, C is 3,...."

Well, for some strange reason, it goes like this: A is 65, B is 66, C is 67,....

These numbers are called the ASCII code of the characters. ASCII is pronounced "ask-key."

The punctuation marks and number digits have ASCII code numbers, too.

ASC( ) Changes Characters into Numbers

Use the ASC( ) function to change characters into ASCII numbers.

Run:

```
REM What number is this key?
PRINT "Press keys to see the ASCII number"
again:
INPUT C$
PRINT C$;TAB(5);ASC(C$)
GO TO again
```

Try out some letters, digits, and punctuation. Hold down SHIFT and press letters.

Press CTRL-C to end the program. Then save it to disk.

CHR$( ) Changes Numbers Into Characters

Use CHR$( ) to change ASCII code numbers into a string holding one character.

Run:

```
REM DISPLAY ASCII
FOR I=0 TO 255
PRINT I, CHR$(I)
PRINT
FOR T=1 TO 200: NEXT T
NEXT I
```

Save the program to disk.

Use CHR$( ) to print the many ASCII characters that are not on the keyboard. They include some mathematics symbols and foreign letters.

CHR$( ) Is the Reverse of ASC( )

We showed these two functions: ASC( ) and CHR$( ).

ASC( ) gives you the ASCII number for the *first* character in the string.

CHR$( ) does the reverse. It gives you the character belonging to each ASCII number.

The ASCII Numbers for Characters

Here are the groups of characters and their ASCII numbers:

0 to	31	control characters for printers
32 to	47	punctuation
48 to	57	number digits
58 to	64	punctuation
65 to	90	capital letters
91 to	96	punctuation
97 to	122	small letters
123 to	127	punctuation
128 to	255	mostly foreign letters

Alphabetical List

ASCII numbers can also help in making alphabetical lists.

Run:

```
REM Alphabetize
PRINT
INPUT "Give me a letter: ",A$
PRINT
INPUT "Give me another: ",B$
PRINT
A=ASC(A$) : B=ASC(B$)
REM Put in alphabetical order by
```

REM seeing which has the lower ASCII number.
IF A>B THEN SWAP A,B : PRINT
PRINT "Here they are in alphabetical order"
PRINT
PRINT CHR$(A);TAB(5);CHR$(B)

The SWAP statement takes any two variables (here A and B) and exchanges their values. It works for strings, too. Try this:

REM Who is first?
m$ = "Macintosh"
a$ = "Amiga"
SWAP m$, a$
PRINT m$, a$

The Mouse Dances on Graph Paper

Enter and save this program to disk:

```
REM --- sketcher ---
   SCREEN 2,640,200,3,2        'high resolution screen
   WINDOW 2,,,,2               'new output window using screen
CALL primarycolors
   COLOR 0,1                   'white forground, black backgnd
   PAINT(0,0),1                'color screen black
   c=0                         'white start color for drawing
   GOSUB message
draw:
   s=MOUSE(0) : x=MOUSE(1) : y=MOUSE(2)
   PSET (x,y),c
   k$=INKEY$   : LOCATE 1,1 : PRINT k$
      IF k$="c" THEN CLS       'clear screen
      IF k$="q" THEN done      'quit program
      IF k$="h" THEN GOSUB message
      IF k$="" THEN k$=" "     'avoid null. gums up PSET
   k=ASC(k$)                   'convert keystroke to number
   IF k$<>" " THEN c=k-48  : IF c>7 THEN c=7
   GOTO draw:
done:                          'graceful exit from program
   WINDOW CLOSE 2              'close the high res window
   WINDOW 1                    'open usual BASIC window
   SCREEN CLOSE 2              'release the hi res memory
END
message:
   LOCATE 1,1
```

```
   PRINT" press h for  HELP"
   PRINT" press c for clear screen"
   PRINT" press numbers Ø - 7 for change of colors"
   PRINT"       1 is black, doesn't show on screen"
   PRINT" press q for  quit"
 RETURN

 SUB primarycolors STATIC
  FOR i=Ø TO 7
   READ r : READ g : READ b : READ c$
   PALETTE i,r,g,b
  NEXT i
  RESTORE
  DATA 1.ØØ, 1.ØØ, 1.ØØ ,white
  DATA Ø.ØØ, Ø.ØØ, Ø.ØØ ,black
  DATA Ø.ØØ, Ø.ØØ, 1.ØØ ,blue
  DATA Ø.ØØ, 1.ØØ, Ø.ØØ ,green
  DATA 1.ØØ, Ø.ØØ, Ø.ØØ ,red
  DATA Ø.ØØ, 1.ØØ, 1.ØØ ,cyan
  DATA 1.ØØ, Ø.ØØ, 1.ØØ ,magenta
  DATA 1.ØØ, 1.ØØ, Ø.ØØ ,yellow
 END SUB
```

The MOUSE( ) function can let you know where the mouse-pointer is on the screen. Then you can use PSET to write a dot there.

The ON-GOTO Statement

Look:

ON K GOTO red, white, blue

If K Is	GOTO
1	red
2	white
3	blue

If K is something else, go to the next line

Instead of GOTO, you can put a GOSUB:

Run:

```
REM counting
FOR I=1 TO 4
ON I GOSUB one, two, three, four
NEXT I
END
one: PRINT" One" : RETURN
two: PRINT" Two, button your shoe": RETURN
three: PRINT" Three" : RETURN
four: PRINT" Four, shut the door" : RETURN
```

After the GOTO or GOSUB, you can put one, two, or as many labels as you want. Each label must belong to a line somewhere in the program.

Assignment 28

1. Write a program which asks for a word. Then it rearranges all the letters in alphabetical order.

2. Write a program that speaks "Double Dutch." It asks for a sentence, then removes all the vowels and prints it out.

3. Add to the sketcher program so that you can use a wider brush to paint with. Let the user enter *b* for *brush* or *d* for *dot*. Use LINE instead of PSET so that a broad brush stroke is drawn instead of a dot.

Instructor Notes 29.   Secret Writing and INKEY$

In this lesson:

1. The INKEY$ and WHILE–WEND statements.
2. Review of the INPUT statement, with and without message.
3. Use for passwords and for character manipulation at input.

INKEY$ requests a single character from the keyboard and puts it into the box of a specified string variable.

There is no screen display at all. No prompt or cursor is displayed, and the keystroke is not echoed to the screen.

One utility of the INKEY$ statement lies just in this fact. For example, a secret password may be received with a series of INKEY$'s without displaying it to bystanders.

Another advantage is that no RETURN key pressing is required. User-friendly programming uses INKEY$ as a simpler way to get single-key user responses. If you need to have the program wait for a keystroke, use the WHILE–WEND statement to wait for a keystroke. This is demonstrated in the lesson.

Because the INKEY$ statement doesn't wait for a key to be pressed, it is suited to action games.

If you want to input numeric values with INKEY$, get them as strings and convert them to numbers using the VAL( ) function discussed in Lesson 27.

Questions

Compare INPUT and INKEY$. For each item, reply INPUT or INKEY$:

(a) Gets whole words and sentences.

(b) Shows a cursor.

(c) Gets one character.

(d) Prints on the screen.

(e) Does not need the RETURN key.

Lesson 29. Secret Writing and INKEY$

There are two ways to use INPUT:

Without a message:

INPUT A$
INPUT N

With a message:

INPUT "Name, age ";Nam$,Age

Either way, the computer waits for you to type a word, sentence, or number.

Then you press the RETURN key to tell the computer that you have finished entering.

The INKEY$ Statement

The INKEY$ statement is different from INPUT. It gets a single character from the keyboard.

It doesn't wait.

It checks to see whether a key is being pressed. If so, it puts the character into the string variable box.

You do not have to press RETURN.

INKEY$ for Invisible Typing

With INKEY$, nothing shows on the screen:

No question mark will show.
No cursor will show.
What you type will not show.

To see what happens, you have to PRINT the variable.

Run:

```
REM Run Away
start:
K$=INKEY$
PRINT K$
GOTO start
```

Press CTRL-C to stop the program.

The computer prints a blank line until you press a key. Then it prints the character.

Try holding down the A key.

See? The computer prints *A*. Then the *A* starts to repeat, and you see a string of letters up the screen.

Making the Computer Wait

In the above program, replace the line

```
K$=INKEY$
```

with

```
key: K$=INKEY$ : IF K$=" " THEN key
```

Now the computer is more polite. It keeps looking until a key is pressed.

WHILE–WEND

Another way to do the same thing is with the statements WHILE and WEND.

Let's rewrite the program:

```
REM Run Away
start:
K$=" "
WHILE K$=" ":K$=INKEY$:WEND
PRINT K$
GOTO start
```

WHILE says stay here as long as K$=" " (no key pressed). So when you press a key, the program moves onto the next line.

As long as K$=" ", the program will continue to do everything between the WHILE and WEND statements. We could have put other statements between WHILE and WEND. Try this:

```
REM Waiting
N$=" "
WHILE N$=" "
PRINT " Please press a key"
PRINT " so I can rest.":PRINT
N$=INKEY$:WEND
PRINT : PRINT
PRINT " Thanks!"
```

Secret Writing

Use INKEY$ in guessing games. You can enter a character without the other player being able to see it.

Run this program:

```
REM secret
start:
PRINT " Press any key"
K$=" ":WHILE K$=" ":K$=INKEY$:WEND
FOR T=1 TO 1000 : NEXT T : BEEP
PRINT " The key you pressed was ";K$
GOTO start
```

Press CTRL-C to end the program.

Making Words of Letters

The INKEY$ statement gets one letter at a time. To make words, glue the strings.

```
REM Get a Secret Word
PRINT " Type a word. End it with a 'RETURN'."
W$=" ":Wback=" "
key:
L$=" ":WHILE L$=" ":L$=INKEY$:WEND
fin: IF ASC(L$) = 13 THEN done
W$=W$ + L$
Wback$=L$ + Wback$ : GOTO key
done:
FOR T=1 TO 3000 : NEXT T
PRINT " Here is the secret word: ";W$
PRINT
PRINT " For fun, here it is backward! ";Wback$
```

How does the computer know when the word is all typed in? Line fin checks whether the RETURN key was pressed. The ASCII number of the RETURN key is 13. It branches to print the word if the RETURN key was pressed.

Assignment 29

1. Write a program that has a menu for the user to choose from. The user makes a choice by typing a single letter. Use INKEY$ to get the letter. Here's an example of a program line to make a menu:

   ```
   PRINT "WHICH COLOR? <R=RED, B=BLUE, G=GREEN>"
   ```

2. Write a sentence making game. Each sentence has a noun subject, a verb, and an object. The first player types a noun (like *The donkey*). The second player types a verb (like *sings*). The third player types another noun (like *the toothpick*). Use INKEY$ so that no player can see the words of the others. You may expand the game by having adjectives before the nouns.

Instructor Notes 30. Logic: AND, OR, NOT

In this lesson:

1. The AND, OR, and NOT relations.
2. True and false are numbers, -1 and 0, respectively.
3. The $=$, $<>$, $<$, $>$, $<=$, and $>=$ signs.

This lesson discusses the AND, OR, and NOT relations and the numeric values for true and false.

Two abstract ideas in this lesson may give difficulty. One is that true and false have numeric values of -1 and 0. Any expression that is of the form of an assertion *(phrase A)*, has a numeric value of 0 or -1. This number is treated just like any other number. It can be stored in a numeric variable, printed, or used in an expression. Most often, it is used in an IF statement.

The other abstract idea compounds the confusion. The IF statement doesn't really look to see whether *phrase A* is present. Rather, it looks for a numeric value between IF and THEN. Any number that is nonzero is treated as true. We call this a little white lie.

You can use the logical values in equations that at first glance look ridiculous. For example,

```
INPUT A
B = 5 - 7*(A<3)
PRINT B
```

The value of B will be 12 or 5 depending on whether A is less than 3 or not.

Questions

1. For each IF statement, tell whether anything will be printed:

```
IF 3=3 THEN PRINT "true1"
IF 3=3 OR 0=2 THEN PRINT "true2"
IF NOT (3=3) THEN PRINT "true3"
IF 3=3 AND 0=2 THEN PRINT "true4"
IF "A"="B" THEN PRINT "true5"
IF NOT ("A"="B") THEN PRINT "true6"
```

2. What numbers will each of these lines print?

```
A=0 : PRINT A; NOT A
A=0 : B=−1 : PRINT A AND B
A=0 : B=0 : PRINT A AND B
A=−1 : B=−1 : PRINT A AND B
A=0 : B=−1 : PRINT A OR B
A=0 : B=0 : PRINT A OR B
A=−1 : B=−1 : PRINT A OR B
PRINT NOT −1
PRINT NOT 0
```

Lesson 30. Logic: AND, OR, NOT

Run:

```
REM AND, OR, NOT
INPUT " Your first name ",n$
PRINT
INPUT " Your age ";age
SAY TRANSLATE$(n$)
ta$=TRANSLATE$("is a teenager")
nta$=TRANSLATE$("is not a teenager")
ss$ =TRANSLATE$("and is sweet sixteen")
jm$ =TRANSLATE$("but just missed")
1 ta=(age>12 AND age<20)
2 IF ta THEN SAY(ta$ )
3 IF NOT ta THEN SAY(nta$)
4 IF age=16 THEN SAY(ss$ )
5 IF age=12 OR age=20 THEN SAY(jm$ )
```

What Does AND Mean?

Two things are true about teenagers: They are over 12 years old and they are less than 20 years old. Look at this line.

IF (you are over 12) AND (you are less than 20) THEN (you are a teenager).

What Does OR Mean?

In this next line, the OR is used. Two things are said: "age is 12" and "age is 20."

Only one of them needs to be true for you to have "just missed" being a teenager.

IF (you are 12) OR (you are 20) THEN (you just missed being a teenager).

True and False Are Numbers

How does the computer do it? It says true and false are numbers.

Rule: True is the number −1.

False is the number 0.

(It is easy to remember that 0 is false because zero is the grade you get if your homework is false.)

To see these numbers, enter this in the immediate mode:

PRINT 3=7

The computer checks to see whether 3 really does equal 7. It doesn't, so it prints a 0, meaning false.

And this:

PRINT 3=3

The computer checks to see whether 3=3. It does, so the computer prints −1, meaning true.

Putting True and False in Boxes

The numbers for true and false are treated just like other numbers. They can be stored in boxes with numeric variable names on the front. Run this:

N = (3=22) : PRINT N

The number 0 is stored in the box N because 3=22 is false.

And this:

N = "B"="B" : PRINT N

The number −1 is stored in the box N because the two letters inside the quotation marks are the same. So the statement "B" = "B" is true.

Whole strings are tested for equality. Run:

PRINT "ab"="ac"

The computer prints 0 for false because the second letters of the two strings are not the same.

The IF Statement Tells Little White Lies

The IF statement looks like this:

IF *(phrase A)* THEN *(statement C)*

Try these in the immediate mode:

IF 0 THEN PRINT "TRUE"

IF −1 THEN PRINT "TRUE"

Now try this:

IF 22 THEN PRINT "TRUE"

What does it print? _____

Rule: In an IF statement, the computer looks at *phrase A*.

If it is zero, the computer says *phrase A* is false and skips what is after THEN.

If it is not zero, the computer says *phrase A* is true and obeys the statement after THEN.

The IF statement tells little white lies. True is supposed to be the number −1, but the IF stretches the truth to say "true is anything that is not false." That is, any number that is not zero is true.

What Does NOT Mean?

NOT changes false to true and true to false. Try this:

```
REM Double Negative
N=0
PRINT "N ";TAB(15);N
PRINT "NOT N";TAB(15);NOT N
PRINT "NOT NOT N ";TAB(15);NOT (NOT N)
' The computer knows that
' "I don't have no..."
' means "I do have ...."
```

Be sure to put a space after each NOT.

The NOT makes sense only when used with 0 or −1. Try this. Change the second line to

    N=−1

It still makes sense. But try

N=3

You do not get true or false as numbers printed. (You do not get −1 or 0.)

The Logical Signs

You can use these six signs in *phrase A*:

=   equal
<> not equal
<   less than
>   greater than
<= less than or equal
>= greater than or equal

You have to press two keys to make the <> sign and the <= and >= signs.

The last two are new, so look at this example to see the difference between < and <=:

2<=3 is true   2<3 is true
3<=3 is true   3<3 is false
4<=3 is false   4<3 is false

These two *phrase A* phrases mean the same:

    2<=Q   (2<Q) OR (2=Q)

Assignment 30

1. Tell what will be found in the box N if:

    N=4=4
    N="G"<>"S"
    N=5>7
    N=3>2 AND 3<2
    N=4=3 OR 4=4
    N=NOT 0
    N=5>=4

2. Tell whether the word JELLYBEAN will be printed:

IF 0	THEN PRINT "JELLYBEAN"
IF −1	THEN PRINT "JELLYBEAN"
IF 9	THEN PRINT "JELLYBEAN"
IF 3<>0	THEN PRINT "JELLYBEAN"
IF 0 OR 1	THEN PRINT "JELLYBEAN"
IF "A"="Z"	THEN PRINT "JELLYBEAN"
IF NOT (0) OR 0	THEN PRINT "JELLYBEAN"
IF 4<=5	THEN PRINT "JELLYBEAN"

3. Write a program to detect a double negative in a sentence. Look for negative words like *not, no, don't, won't, can't, nothing,* and count them. If there are two such words, there is a double negative. Test the program on this sentence: COMPUTERS AIN'T GOT NO BRAINS.

Instructor Notes 31. STOP, CONT, Debugging

In this lesson:

1. The STOP statement.
2. The CONT command.
3. Compare ways to start or restart a program: RUN, GOTO, CONT.
4. How to debug a program.

STOP and CONT help in debugging a program. Proper use of CTRL-C, GOTO, delay loops, and the PRINT statement also contributes to bug squashing.

An inexperienced programmer feels hopeless inertia when a program doesn't work right. Rather than sitting and staring, it is more useful to try some changes. Any changes are better than none, but random changes are very inefficient. The best changes are those that eliminate sections of the program from the list of possible hiding places for the bug.

Debugging uses certain tricks to help systematically isolate a bug and puzzle out what is wrong. Delay loops slow down the program so that you can see what is happening. PRINT statements give the values of a variable. STOP statements halt the program at strategic points so that you can puzzle for as long as you want before continuing. After the bug is found and corrected, remove these helping statements from the program.

Don't overlook those techniques you can use after the program is stopped with CTRL-C, STOP, or END. You can PRINT out any variable values you like in order to see what the program has done. You can also do arithmetic in the PRINT statement to check what the program should be doing. You can even use LET in the immediate mode to change variable values before CONTinuing the run.

Lesson 17 showed how the Trace On option from the Run menu helps in stepping through the program faster than manual stepping with the A-T keys. Now we show how the TRON and TROFF statements allow you to pick which parts of the program to subject to the trace. This allows you to skip tracing in those parts of the program that are okay, and so speeds up the debugging task.

As programs grow in complexity, more of the bugs result from unforeseen interactions between separate parts of the program. Lesson 32 treats modular programming and other schemes for helping make programs easier to understand and therefore easier to debug.

Questions

1. How are the STOP statement and CTRL-C keys different?

2. Can you pick in which line CTRL-C will stop the program? Can you pick with the STOP statement?

3. How are the STOP and END statements different?

4. What does the CONT command do?

5. Why would you put STOP statements in your program?

6. How do delay loops help you debug a program?

7. How do extra PRINT statements help you debug a program?

8. Why do you remove the STOP and extra PRINT statements from the program after you have fixed the errors?

Lesson 31. STOP, CONT, Debugging

The STOP Statement

Enter and run:

```
REM Secret STOP
RANDOMIZE TIMER
N=FIX(RND*199)
FOR I=1 TO 200
IF I=N THEN STOP
NEXT I
PRINT" Done"
```

The program will stop, and the computer will print

OK

The STOP statement stopped the computer when I was equal to N. So the PRINT" Done" statement was not reached. The program is not really over. You can start it again. But wait.

What do you suppose the secret value of I was?

Enter in immediate mode:

PRINT I

The CONT Command Starts the Program Again

Enter the command CONT. Try it.

This time, the program starts at I=N and continues until the loop is finished. Then the program prints

Done

STOP Is Like END

STOP makes the computer stop and enter the immediate mode.

It is like END, except you can CONTinue after a STOP statement, but not after an END statement. Try changing STOP to END in the above program and repeat the CONT command after the program runs and stops. (You will get a Can't continue error message. Click the left button in the Ok box.)

You can have as many STOP statements in your program as you like.

STOP is used for debugging your program.

Another Way to Stop the Program

Remember, you can stop running the program with the CTRL-C keys.

Enter:

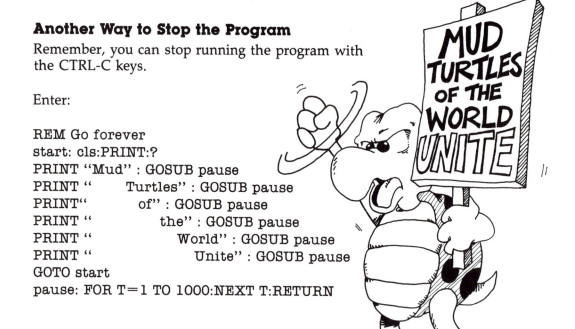

```
REM Go forever
start: cls:PRINT:?
PRINT "Mud" : GOSUB pause
PRINT "    Turtles" : GOSUB pause
PRINT"      of" : GOSUB pause
PRINT "        the" : GOSUB pause
PRINT "          World" : GOSUB pause
PRINT "            Unite" : GOSUB pause
GOTO start
pause: FOR T=1 TO 1000:NEXT T:RETURN
```

Run it. Press CTRL-C. This stops the program wherever it is. It prints

Ok

and enters the immediate mode. The CONT command starts the program again at the same spot.

The trouble with stopping most programs this way is that you do not know where in the program the computer is.

Why STOP?

You put STOP in whatever part of your program is not working right. Then you run the program. After it stops, you look to see what happened.

(Or you use CTRL-C to stop the program, but it may not stop in the spot where the trouble is.)

Put on your thinking cap. Ask yourself questions about what happened as the program ran.

You are in the immediate mode. You can:

List parts of the program and study them.

Use the PRINT statement to look at variables. Do they have the values you expected?

Do little calculations on the computer in the "calculator mode" (another name for the immediate mode) to check what the computer is doing.

Use the LET statement to change the values of variables.

If you find the trouble, you may add lines, change lines, or delete lines.

Review of Stopping and Starting

The three ways to stop a program are STOP, END, and CTRL-C.

There are four ways to start a program:

RUN   your old friend
RUN XX   where XX is a line number or label
GOTO XX   where XX is a line number or label
CONT   if you have not changed the program

What is the difference between these four ways?

CONT and GOTO XX use whatever values are currently in the variable boxes.

CONT starts at the line where STOP or CTRL-C stopped the program. GOTO XX starts at line XX.

You may use the CONT command if you have not

added a line,
deleted a line,
or changed a line by editing it.

RUN and RUN XX throw away all the current variable boxes.

RUN starts at the first line of the program; RUN XX starts at line XX.

Debugging

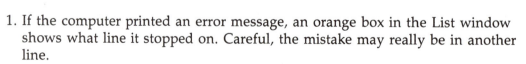

Little errors in your program are called bugs.

Here is a list of items that will help you figure out what is wrong when your program doesn't run right.

1. If the computer printed an error message, an orange box in the List window shows what line it stopped on. Careful, the mistake may really be in another line.

2. If the computer just keeps running, but doesn't do the right thing, stop it and put some PRINT statements in that will tell what is happening.

3. Or you can put STOP statements in the program.

4. If the program runs so fast that you can't tell what is happening, put in some delay loops to slow it down.

5. Use the Trace On choice from the Run menu. Or you can put a TRON statement at the beginning of the spot in your program that is giving you trouble. Put a TROFF statement at the end of the messy spot.

After you have found and fixed the program, take the PRINTs, the STOPs, the delay loops, and the TROFF and TRON statements out of the program.

Assignment 31

Practice debugging. Write a program that has some loops and a lot of PRINT and STOP statements and delay loops in it. When it stops (from STOP, END, or CTRL-C), print out some variable results in the immediate mode and modify the variables with LET statements. Try starting the program with CONT, RUN, RUN XX, and GOTO XX. Keep trying things until you understand how these commands help in debugging.

Instructor Notes 32. Clear, Friendly Programs

In this lesson:

1. Users need a smooth-running program.
2. A programmer wants clear listings.
3. An outline for medium- and large-size programs.
4. Offering instructions and giving prompts.
5. Avoid scrolling. Use LOCATE and erase old writing.
6. Avoid the RETURN key. Use INKEY$.
7. Use UCASE$ to avoid uncertainty about capital and small letters.
8. Trapping errors upon input.

This lesson shows how to write clear programs which interact with the user in a friendly way.

Programs should be clearly structured from a programmer's point of view, and spaghetti programs should be avoided. This lesson presents a format for writing programs. While methods of imposing order on the task are largely a matter of taste, the methods used here can serve to introduce the ideas.

User-friendly programming requires more than opening a bag of tricks. Success depends mostly on the attitude of the programmer. "Turn your annoyance detectors up to high" as you write and debug the program. Play the part of the users and try to anticipate difficulties they will have.

Make your screen displays easy to read. Avoid scrolling. Place the cursor with LOCATE and print what you want. Then, when done, erase by again placing the cursor with LOCATE and print a string of blanks.

Use INKEY$ whenever your user must input a single keystroke (as in answering a question with Y or N). This saves the annoyance of having to press the RETURN key.

Trap errors. When asking for a number in a given range, or for certain letters or words, check that the input satisfies the conditions. If not, make the user try again.

When you call for a complicated set of inputs, let the user enter the whole set. Then ask if entries are okay. If they're not, give an opportunity to fix things.

Questions

1. Should your program give instructions whether the user wants them or not?

2. What is a main loop? What does it do?

3. What is an error trap? How would you trap errors if you asked your user to enter a number from 1 to 5?

4. In what part of the program are most of the GOSUB statements found?

5. How do you avoid scrolling too much?

6. How do you help the user if he or she accidentally puts the CAPS LOCK key down?

7. Why put the "starting stuff" section of the program at the end of the program?

Lesson 32. Clear, Friendly Programs

There are two kinds of users:

1. Most want to *run* the program. They need:

   instructions
   prompts
   clear writing on the screen
   no clutter on the screen
   erasing old stuff from the screen
   not too much key pressing
   protection from their own errors

2. Some want to *change* the program. They need:

   a program made in parts
   each part with a title in a REM
   explanations in the program

Don't forget that you are a user of your own programs, too. Be kind to yourself.

Programs Have Four Parts

1. Starting stuff (at the beginning of the program run)

   gives instructions to the user
   draws a screen display
   sets variables to their starting values
   asks the user for starting information

2. Main loop

   controls the order in which tasks
     are done
   calls subroutines to do the tasks

3. Subroutines and subprograms

   perform parts of the program

4. Description

   tells the user about the program

Program Outline

```
REM program name

desc:  'description
       'REMs that give a description of the
       'program, variable names, and so forth

main:  'main loop
       'calls subroutines
       END

sub1:  'subroutines
       'subroutines go here
       RETURN

sub2:  'second subroutine
       RETURN

init:  'starting stuff
       'asks for starting information
       'sets variable values, DIMensions arrays
       'gives instrucvions
       GOTO main

subprog1:
       'subprograms are MERGEd to the end
       END SUB
```

Put a Description at the Beginning

A programmer reads your listing to understand the program and perhaps to modify it. The description tells how the program works and what the variable names mean.

Put the Main Loop Next

The main loop is an outline of the program. Put it near the front. It shows what subroutines and subprograms are used.

The subroutines do most of the work. The programmer wants to read them carefully to see what happens.

Put Starting Stuff at the End

The starting stuff gets the program started. It gives help and instructions, asks the user questions, DIMensions arrays, stores initial values of variables, and holds DATA statements and strings.

It may be the biggest part of the program. Although it contains many important details, it does not help the reader very much to understand the outline of the program. Put it out of the way near the back.

Information Please

PRINT "Do you want instructions <y/n> "

This lets a beginner see instructions and lets others say no.

Tie a String Around the User's Finger

Use a prompt to remind users what choices they have.

In this example:

<y/n>

the choice is y for yes or n for no.

Beginners need long prompts. Other users like short prompts.

Don't Give the User a Headache

Scrolling gives headaches.

BASIC usually scrolls. It writes new lines at the bottom of the screen and pushes old lines up.

It is like the scrolls the Romans used for writing. They unwound from the bottom and wound up at the top.

Avoid scrolling. Use LOCATE to print just where you want. Erase by printing a string of blanks to the same spot.

Use delay loops to keep the writing on the screen while the user reads it.

Ouch! My Fingers Hurt

Use INKEY$ to enter single letters. This saves having to press RETURN.

```
PRINT "Do you need instructions? <y/n> "
key1:
R$=" ":WHILE R$=" ":R$=INKEY$:WEND
IF R$="y" THEN inst
```

Watch Out for the CAPS LOCK Key

Just when you expect the user to enter small letters, uppercase are used. Use the UCASE$( ) statement to fix this problem. So the last line above is better written as

IF UCASE$(R$)="Y" THEN inst

Set Traps for Errors

Add this line below the other three lines:

IF UCASE$(R$)<>"N" THEN key1

You gave the user only two choices, y and n. Send the user back for another chance if you do not get an answer you want.

Traps make your program bombproof so that users will be unable to goof it up.

Sensible Numbers

old: INPUT" Your age,"age
IF age<0 OR age>120 THEN old

Test user inputs to see whether the numbers make sense. If not, there is an error, and the user should try again.

Assignment 32

1. Make a program to write a very large number, 50 digits. Pick the digits at random. Put a comma between each set of 3 digits.

2. Write a secret cipher program. The user chooses a password and makes a cipher alphabet like this:

If the password is DRAGONETTE, remove the repeated letters, get DRAGONET, put it at the front of the alphabet and the rest of the letters after it in normal order.

DRAGONETBCFHIJKLMPQSUVWXYZ   cipher alphabet

ABCDEFGHIJKLMNOPQRSTUVWXYZ   normal alphabet

The user chooses to code or decode from a menu.

Appendices

Disk Usage

As the instructions that came with the Amiga state, you should make copies of the Kickstart and Workbench disks packed with your computer. You should never use the originals for everyday tasks. Make one or more copies for working disks and put aside the originals for making backups. The manual that came with the Amiga explains how to make copies of disks.

Prepare a copy of Workbench for the exclusive use of your student. We will call this copy of Workbench the "Studentdisk".

This Studentdisk will also have room to hold the Amiga BASIC files from the Extras disk. This means that booting the computer will involve only two disks, a copy of Kickstart and the Studentdisk, rather than the three disks mentioned in Lesson 1: Kickstart, Workbench, and Extras. And all your student's programs can be saved to the Studentdisk.

Warning: Never remove a disk from the disk drive until the *red drive light goes out*. The temptation to remove a disk early is great, because the screen may indicate that you are done with the current step and should remove the disk, but the red light is not yet out. *Ignore the screen and watch for the red light to go out.*

Starting the System

Begin by placing your copy of the Kickstart disk into the slot of the computer (metal end in and metal disk side down). Turn on the computer. After the disk drive makes a few grunts, the screen shows a hand holding a Workbench disk (upside down) as a reminder to remove Kickstart and insert the Workbench disk in the drive (in this case, insert Studentdisk).

After Workbench finishes loading, the title bar says (in the 512K version computer with Workbench release 1.1)

Workbench release 1.1: 426576 free memory

and shows a disk icon with Workbench written under it.

Two Disks at Once

Now take the Studentdisk with Workbench on it out and insert the Extras disk. The Extras icon appears. It may even partly cover the Studentdisk icon. This does no harm, but you can move the Extras icon by moving the arrow onto the icon, holding the *left* button down, moving the red disk to a nearby spot, and releasing the button. The Extras icon jumps to the new location and remains black. Fine. Now double-click the *left* button on the Extras icon, and its window will be loaded to the screen.

Copying Amiga BASIC

Find the Amiga BASIC icon in the Extras window. Place the pointer so that it is on the Amiga BASIC icon. Press and hold down the *left* button. Now draw the mouse while continuing to hold down the *left* button so the encircled X is squarely over the Extras disk icon; release the *left* button. You are telling the system to copy Amiga BASIC to the Studentdisk. You'll need to insert and remove disks a few times; follow the instructions that appear on the screen. Remember not to remove a disk while the red light is on.

Loading BASIC

Now reload the Studentdisk window by double-clicking the Studentdisk icon. This time the Amiga BASIC icon appears in the window, but probably on top of the other icons. Clean up the window by selecting (*right* button) the Clean Up choice from the Special menu.

Now double-click on the BASIC icon to load BASIC.

You see the familiar BASIC and List windows.

BASIC Reserved Words

*Reserved words discussed in this book are in **bold**.*

ABS
ALL
AND
APPEND
AREA
AREAFILL
AS
ASC
ATN

BASE
BEEP
BREAK

CALL
CDBL
CHAIN
CHDIR
CHR$
CINT
CIRCLE
CLEAR
CLNG
CLOSE
CLS
COLLISION
COLOR
COMMON
CONT
COS
CSNG
CSRLIN
CVD
CVI
CVL
CVS

DATA
DATE$
DECLARE
DEF
DEFDBL
DEFINT
DEFLNG
DEFSNG
DEFSTR
DELETE
DIM

ELSE
ELSE IF
END
EOF
EQV
ERASE
ERL
ERR
ERROR
EXIT
EXP

FIELD
FILES
FIX
FN
FOR
FRE
FUNCTION

GET
GOSUB
GOTO

HEX$

IF
IMP
INKEY$
INPUT
INSTR
INT

KILL

LBOUND
LEFT$
LEN
LET
LIBRARY
LINE
LIST
LLIST
LOAD
LOC
LOCATE
LOF
LOG
LPOS
LPRINT
LSET

MENU
MERGE
MID$
MKD$
MKI$
MKL$
MKS$
MOD
MOUSE

NAME
NEW
NEXT
NOT

OBJECT
OCT$
OFF
ON
OPEN
OPTION BASE
OR
OUTPUT

PAINT
PALETTE
PATTERN
PEEK
PEEKL
PEEKW
POINT
POKE
POKEL
POKEW
POS
PRESET
PRINT
PSET
PTAB
PUT

RANDOMIZE
READ
REM
RESET
RESTORE
RESUME
RETURN
RIGHT$

RND
RSET
RUN

SADD
SAVE
SAY
SCREEN
SCROLL
SGN
SHARED
SIN
SLEEP
SOUND
SPACE$
SPC
SQR
STATIC
STEP
STICK
STOP
STR$
STRIG
STRING$
SUB
SWAP
SYSTEM

TAB
TAN
THEN
TIME$
TIMER
TO
TRANSLATE$
TROFF
TRON

UBOUND
UCASE$
USING
USR

VAL
VARPTR

WAIT
WAVE
WEND
WHILE
WIDTH
WINDOW
WRITE

XOR

Glossary

argument
The variable, number, or string that appears in the parentheses of a function.

INT(N)   has   N   as an argument.
LEN(W$)   has   W$ as an argument.

array
A set of variables that have the same name. The members of the array are numbered. The numbers appear in parentheses after the variable name. *See also* subscript.

A(0)   is the first member of the array A.
B$(7)   is the eighth member of the array B$.
CD(3,M+1)   is a member of the array CD.

arrow keys
The four keys on the computer that have arrows on them. They move the input cursor to the left and right, and up and down.

ASCII
Stands for American Standard Code for Information Interchange. Each character has an ASCII number.

assertion
The name of a phrase that can be true or false. The *phrase A* in an IF statement is an assertion. An assertion has a numeric value of 0 or -1. *See also* expression, false, logic, phrase A, true.

The assertion   "A"<>"B"   is true.
The assertion   3 = 4   is false.

background
The part of the screen that is blank, not having characters on it.

BASIC

Beginners's All-purpose Symbolic Instruction Code. A computer language originated by John Kemeny and Thomas Kurtz at Dartmouth College in the early 1960s.

blank

The character that is a space.

branch

A point in a program where there is a choice of which statement to execute next. An IF statement is a branch. So is an ON-GOTO statement. A branch is not the same as a jump where there is no choice. *See also* jump.

buffer

A storage area in memory for temporary storage of information being input or output from the computer.

button

The mouse has two buttons. Pushing the right button shows the menu bar. Moving the mouse arrow on a menu word shows the choices you have under that menu word, and releasing the right button selects one of those choices. The left button controls loading files by double-clicking on an icon, moving the cursor in the List window, and editing (Cut, Save, and Paste) from the Edit menu when in the List window.

call

Using a GOSUB calls the subroutine. You can call a subprogram by giving its name, or by using CALL followed by its name. Putting a function in a statement calls the function. Call means that the computer goes and performs the commands in the subroutine or subprogram. Then it returns to the calling spot.

carriage return

On a typewriter, you push the lever that moves the carriage carrying the paper so a new line can begin. In computing, it means the cursor is moved to the start of the line, but not down to the next line. *See also* CRLF, linefeed.

character

Letters, digits, punctuation marks, and the space are characters.

checksum

In some I/O operations, the computer adds together all the character numbers. The resulting sum is the checksum. If the data was transmitted correctly, the checksum calculated after the data is received will agree with that calculated before the data was sent. *See also* I/O.

clear

To erase. Used in "clear the screen" and "clear memory."

column

Things arranged vertically. *See also* row.

command

In BASIC, a command makes the computer do some action, such as LOAD a program or clear memory with NEW. *See also* expression, statement. Some commands need expressions to be complete:

SAVE "myprogram"

concatenation

Sticking two strings together.

constant

A number or string that does not change as the program runs. It is stored right in the program line, not in a box with a name on the front. *See also* line.

CRLF

Short for Carriage Return followed by Line Feed. On a typewriter, this is just called a carriage return. *See also* carriage return, linefeed.

cursor

A marker that shows where the next character on the screen or in a storage buffer will be placed. Cursor means "runner." The cursor runs along the screen as you type. There are two kinds of cursors in the Amiga computer:

Input cursor   A flashing line on the screen.
PRINT cursor   Invisible; "shows" where next character will be printed.

data

BASIC has two kinds of data: numeric and string. Logical data (true, false) is a type of numeric data.

debug

To run a program so that you can find the errors and fix them. You fix the errors by editing the program. *See also* edit.

delay loop

A part of the program that just uses up time and does nothing else.

FOR T=1 TO 2000:NEXT T

duration

A number in a SOUND statement that tells how long the sound will last.

edit

To retype parts of a program to correct it.

enable

To make a window active. You do this by clicking on the left mouse button while the pointer is inside the window.

enter

To put information into the computer by typing, then pushing the RETURN key. The information goes into the input buffer as it is typed. When RETURN is pressed, the computer uses the information.

erase

To destroy information in memory or write blanks to the screen. *See also* clear.

error trap

Part of a program that checks for mistakes in information that the user has entered, or checks to see whether computed results are within reasonable bounds.

execute
To run a program or to perform a single command or statement.

expression
A portion of a statement that has a single value, either a number or a string. *See also* value.

7*X+1
"DOPE "<> N$
A$ + "HAT"

false
The number 0. *See also* assertion, logic, true.

fork in the road
A branch point in the program. *See also* branch.

function
BASIC has a number of functions built in. Each function has a name followed by arguments. The function has a single value (numeric or string) determined by its arguments. *See also* argument, value. The functions treated in this book are

ASC, CHR$, FIX, LEFT$, LEN, MID$,
RIGHT$, RND, STR$, VAL, TAB, TIMER,
TRANSLATE$, UCASE$

gadget
A little spot on a window that does certain things when you click a mouse button in it. Here are some of the gadgets: the lower right corner is a sizing gadget, the upper right corner is a foreground-background gadget, the upper left corner is an erase window gadget, and the top bar of the window is a moving gadget. Also possible are scroll gadgets on the edges of the window.

garbage
A random mess of characters in memory. Usually due to human or machine error.

graphics
Picture drawing.

icon
A little picture in a window that stands for the name of a file. You can load the file by double-clicking the left mouse button. *See also* button, mouse.

index
An array name is followed by one or more numbers or numeric variables inside parentheses. Each number is an index. Another word for index is *subscript*.

Q(7,J)   7 and J are indices.

integers
The whole numbers, positive, negative and zero.

I/O
Input/Output. Input from keyboard, disk, etc. Output to screen, printer, disk, etc.

jump
The GOTO statement makes the computer jump to another line in the program rather than execute the next line.

Kickstart
A program loaded from the Kickstart disk when you first turn on your Amiga. Kickstart is needed to boot the system. As soon as Kickstart is loaded, it shows a picture of the Workbench disk, meaning you must put it in the drive to continue booting the system.

line
Lines may start with a label (followed by a colon) or a line number. The line proper starts with a statement which may have expressions, arguments, and so forth, following it. The line may end at that point, or it may have a colon with another statement.

Parts of a line:

tz: IF 7<=INT(Z) THEN PRINT LEN(Q$+"R")+2;"RAT":GOTO 40

tz:	label
IF 7<=INT(Z) THEN PRINT..."RAT"	statement
GOTO 40	statement
7<=INT(Z)	assertion
7<=INT(Z)	expression
LEN (Q$+"R")+2;"RAT"	expression
INT(Z)	function
LEN(Q$)	function
Z	argument
Q$+"R"	argument
7, "R," 2, "RAT"	constants
<=, +	operations
IF, INT, THEN, PRINT, LEN, GOTO	reserved words

line buffer
The storage space that receives the characters you type in. *See also* buffer.

linefeed
To move the cursor straight down to the next line. The ASCII number 10 signals this command to the screen or printer. *See also* carriage return, CRLF.

line label
A word followed by a colon that begins a line and names it. Programmers generally label (or number) only some lines, for example, those heading a module in the program or lines that are targets of GOTO, GOSUB, etc.

line number
A number (in place of a label) at the beginning of a program line.

listing
A list of all the lines in a program.

load

To transfer the information in a file on disk to the memory of the computer by using the LOAD command.

logic

The part of a program that compares numbers or strings. The relations =, <>, <, >, <=, and >= are used. *See also* assertion, phrase A.

loop

A part of the program that is done over and over again. There are many kinds of loops: FOR-NEXT and WHILE–WEND are two examples of loops discussed in this book.

loop variable

The number that changes as the loop is repeated.

```
FOR I=1 TO 5
NEXT I
```

memory

The part of the computer where information is stored. Memory is made of semi-conductor chips, but we think of it as "boxes" with labels on the front and information inside.

menu

Pull-down menus come as part of the Amiga screen style.

Homemade menus are a list of choices shown on the screen. Each choice has a letter or number beside it. The program user presses a key to pick which choice is wanted.

message

A statement that tells what is expected in an INPUT statement.

```
INPUT "AGE";A
```

monitor
(1) We use it to mean a box with a TV-type screen that is connected to the computer which displays text and graphics. It is different from a TV in that it cannot receive TV signals directly. (2) In machine language programming, a monitor is a control program.

mouse
A device with a ball on the underside. Moving it on the table moves an arrow on the screen. The mouse has two buttons. *See also* button.

nesting
When one thing is inside another. In a program, we nest loops. Inside a statement, we can nest expressions or functions.

```
L=INT(LEN(P$)+3)      nested functions
X=5*(6+(7*(8+K)))     nested parentheses
```

```
FOR i=1 TO 10
FOR j=1 TO 5:NEXT j   nested loop
NEXT i
```

number
One type of information in BASIC. The other is string. The numbers are generally decimal numbers. *See also* integers, string.

operation
In arithmatic: addition, subtraction, multiplication, and division, with symbols $+$, $-$, $*$, and $/$. The only operation for strings is concatenation ($+$).

phrase A
In this book, the name given to an assertion in an IF statement. *See also* assertion.

```
IF A>4 THEN 500
A>4 is "phrase A"
```

pitch
The number in a SOUND statement that tells the musical pitch of the sound. The pitch can be high or low.

pixel
Picture element. The smallest dot that is placed on the screen in graphics.

pointer
A number in memory that tells where in a list of DATA you are at the present moment.

program
A list of lines containing statements. The computer executes the statements in order when the RUN command is entered. The program is stored in a special part of memory. Only one program can be stored at a time.

prompt
A little message you put on the screen with an INPUT to remind the user what kind of answer you expect. Its name comes from the hint that actors in a play get from the prompter if they forget their lines.

pseudorandom number
A number that is calculated in secret by the computer using the RND function. It is usually called a *random number*. Pseudorandom emphasizes that the number really is not random (since it is calculated by a known method), but is just not predictable by the user of the computer.

punctuation
The characters such as period, comma, /, ?, !.

random numbers
Numbers that cannot be predicted, like the numbers that show after the roll of dice, or the number of heads you get in tossing a coin ten times.

remark
A comment you make in the program by putting it in a REM statement. The computer ignores REM statements.

```
REM the graphics setup subroutine
' Used instead of the word REM
```

reserved words
A list of words and abbreviations that BASIC recognizes as commands, statements, or functions. Reserved words cannot be used as variable names.

return a value
When a function is used (called), its spot in the expression is replaced with a value (a number or a string). This is called *returning a value.*

row
Things arranged horizontally (across). *See also* column.

RUN mode
The action of the computer when it is executing a program is called *operating in the RUN mode.* You get into the RUN mode from the immediate mode by entering RUN. When the computer ends the program for any reason, it returns to the immediate mode.

save
To put the program that is in the computer's memory on disk.

screen
The monitor screen (similar to a TV screen) that is hooked up to the computer. *See also* monitor.

scrolling
The usual way the computer writes to the screen is to put the new line below the previously printed line. When the last screen line is printed, all the old lines are moved up and the text on the top line disappears from the display. This is called *scrolling.*

simple variable
A variable that is not an array variable.

stack
A data type used in machine language programming. The data elements are arranged in a column and the last one put on is the first one taken off.

starting stuff

The name given in this book to initialization material in a program. It includes REMs for describing the program, input of initial values of variables, setup of array dimensions, drawing screen graphics, and any other things that need to be done just once at the beginning of a program run.

statement

An instruction in a program is usually called a statement.

string

A type of data in BASIC. It consists of a row of characters. *See also* number.

subroutine

A section of a program that starts with a line called from a GOSUB statement and ends with a RETURN statement. It may be called from more than one place in the program.

subscript

Another name for *index*. A number in the parentheses of an array. It tells which member of the array is being used. *See also* index.

syntax

The way a statement in BASIC is spelled. A syntax error means that the spelling of a statement, command, function, or variable name is wrong, the punctuation is wrong, or the order of parts in the line is wrong.

timing loop

A loop that does nothing except use up a certain amount of time. *See also* delay loop.

title

The name of a program or subroutine. Put it in a REM statement.

true

Has the value -1. *See also* assertion, false, logic.

type
To press keys on the computer. Typing is different from entering. *See also* enter.

value
The value of a variable is the number or string stored in the memory box belonging to the variable. *See also* variable.

variable
A value which can be changed while the program is running. Each variable is stored in a box in memory which is reserved for that variable. The box holds a value. When the computer sees a variable name in an expression, it goes to the box and takes a copy of what is in the box back to the expression and puts it where the variable name was. Then it continues to evaluate the expression. *See also* variable name.

variable, array
See array.

variable, simple
See simple variable.

variable name
A variable is either a string variable or a numeric variable. The name tells which. String variables have names ending in a dollar sign ($). Numeric variables do not.

window
A portion of the screen (or all of it) with a border which shows some kind of output. Windows have gadgets in the corners and may show icons. They may have a title at the top. The screen may also show a menu in the title bar, but this is not part of the window because different windows may show the same menu. Windows can change size, and one window may partly or completely cover another window. *See also* gadget, icon.

Workbench
The operating system you see on the screen in the form of windows and icons. It is loaded from the Workbench disk after the Kickstart disk is loaded. You need Workbench in the computer to do any other task.

Answers to Selected Assignments

Lesson 2

```
REM Names
PRINT "Minda"
PRINT "Anne"
PRINT "Carlson"


REM --- birds ---
CLS
PRINT
BEEP
PRINT "---o---"
PRINT
BEEP
PRINT "          \o/"
PRINT
BEEP
PRINT "   --o--"
```

Lesson 4

```
REM ((( smile )))
COLOR Ø,1
PALETTE 3,1,Ø,Ø
CLS
PRINT
PRINT
PRINT
COLOR 3,1
PRINT "          oo      oo"
PRINT "          oo      oo"
PRINT
PRINT
COLOR Ø,1
PRINT "      *            *  "
PRINT "       *          *  "
PRINT "        ***************  "
```

Lesson 5

```
REM --- talking ---
  CLS
  SAY TRANSLATE$("Hello. What is your name?")
  INPUT N$
  SAY TRANSLATE$("Well"+N$+"it is silly to talk to computers")
END


REM --- In the Box ---
CLS
PRINT" What is your favorite color?"
INPUT C$
PRINT
PRINT" I put that in the box C$."
PRINT
PRINT" Now, what is your favorite animal?"
INPUT C$
PRINT
PRINT" I put that in box C$ also."
PRINT
PRINT" Now let's see what is in box C$."
PRINT
PRINT" It is "
PRINT C$
```

Lesson 6

```
REM --- Music ---
CLS
PRINT " What is your favorite musical group?"
INPUT g$
CLS
PRINT " What tune do they play?"
INPUT t$
CLS
PRINT
PRINT g$;" plays ";t$
```

Lesson 7

```
REM <<< Feelings >>>
SAY TRANSLATE$(" How is the wether?")
      REM  weather is misspelled so it will sound better
INPUT w$
SAY TRANSLATE$(" And how do you feel?")
INPUT f$
a$="You mean"+w$+"and"+f$
SAY TRANSLATE$(a$)
```

Lesson 8

```
REM === Teen Power ===
COLOR Ø,1
CLS
start:
  PRINT " T E E N    P O W E R "
    PRINT
    PRINT
    PRINT
GOTO start
REM press CTRL-C to end the program
REM enter COLOR 1,Ø to restore white on blue screen
```

Lesson 9

```
REM +++ Color  Guessing  Game +++
CLS
SAY TRANSLATE$(" Player 1 turn your back")
SAY TRANSLATE$(" Player 2 enter a color")
INPUT c$
CLS
SAY TRANSLATE$(" Player 1 turn around and guess")
guess:
INPUT g$
IF g$<>c$ THEN SAY TRANSLATE$(" Wrong, try again")
IF g$= c$ THEN SAY TRANSLATE$(" Right          ")
IF g$<>c$ THEN GOTO guess
```

Lesson 10

```
REM ***** Birth Year *****
CLS
PRINT " How old are you?                    "
INPUT a
PRINT " And what year is this?              "
INPUT y
b=y-a
PRINT " Has you birthday come yet this year. "
PRINT " <y/n>"
key1:      INPUT y$
IF y$= "y" THEN   answer
IF y$<>"n" THEN   key1
b=b-1
answer:
PRINT " You were born in ";b;"."


REM ***** Multiplication *****
    CLS
    PRINT
PRINT " Give me a number."
INPUT A
    PRINT
PRINT " Give me another."
INPUT B
    PRINT
C=A * B
PRINT " Here is their product: ";C
```

Lesson 11

```
REM ::::: Nicknames :::::
    CLS
SAY TRANSLATE$(" What is your last name?       ")
    PRINT
INPUT Last$
    CLS
SAY TRANSLATE$(" Someone type the nickname.    ")
    PRINT
INPUT Nick$
    CLS
    FOR t=1 TO 5000 : NEXT t
SAY TRANSLATE$(" You are called:"+ Nick$ + Last$)
PRINT TAB(5);Last$;TAB(15);Nick$
```

```
REM ..... s l o w   p o k e .....
    CLS
    PRINT
    BEEP
    FOR t=1 TO 2000:NEXT t
  SAY TRANSLATE$("i am")
    BEEP
    FOR t=1 TO 2000:NEXT t
  SAY TRANSLATE$("very")
    BEEP
    FOR t=1 TO 2000:NEXT t
  SAY TRANSLATE$("very")
    BEEP
    FOR t=1 TO 2000:NEXT t
  SAY TRANSLATE$("sleepy")
```

Lesson 12

```
REM +++ I Got Your Number +++
 another:
  CLS : PRINT
  PRINT" Give me a number between zero and ten:" : PRINT
  INPUT N : PRINT
    IF N<0 OR N>10 THEN another
    IF N=0 THEN PRINT" I got plenty of nothing.
    IF N=1 THEN PRINT" I'm number one!"
    IF N=2 THEN PRINT" Two is company."
    IF N=3 THEN PRINT" Three's a crowd."
    IF N=4 THEN PRINT" A foursome!"
    IF N=5 THEN PRINT" Five Alive."
    IF N=6 THEN PRINT" Six flags."
    IF N=7 THEN PRINT" Lucky seven."
    IF N=8 THEN PRINT" Eight is enough."
    IF N=9 THEN PRINT" Nine lives."
    IF N=10 THEN PRINT" Ten gallon hat!"
    PRINT:PRINT "Another?":INPUT y$
    IF y$="yes" THEN another
  PRINT " That's all, folks"
```

Lesson 13

```
REM ^^^ Roll Dem Bones ^^^
  CLS : PRINT
  RANDOMIZE TIMER
  a$=" Roll the dice"
again:
  CLS : PRINT : PRINT
  LET d1=1+FIX(RND*6)
  LET d2=1+FIX(RND*6)
  LET d =d1+d2
  SAY TRANSLATE$(a$)
  PRINT : PRINT :PRINT
  PRINT a$
  PRINT TAB(15);"The first  die ";d1
  PRINT TAB(15);"The second die ";d2
  PRINT TAB(15);"The dice show  ";d
  SAY TRANSLATE$("The first  die shows"+STR$(d1))
  SAY TRANSLATE$("The second die shows"+STR$(d2))
  SAY TRANSLATE$("The dice show       "+STR$(d ))
  PRINT" Another roll? <y/n>"
  INPUT y$
  IF UCASE$(y$)="Y" THEN again
END


REM >>> Paper, Scissors, Rock >>>
  CLS : PRINT : PRINT  : PRINT
  RANDOMIZE TIMER
  PRINT TAB(19)"  Play the "
  PRINT
  PRINT TAB(19);"     P a p e r "            : PRINT
  PRINT TAB(19);"        S c i s s o r s " : PRINT
  PRINT TAB(19);"           R o c k      " : PRINT
  PRINT
  PRINT TAB(19);" Game against the computer!"
  PRINT
  PRINT" Enter 'Q' to end the game."
  PRINT
  PRINT" Enter your choice <p,s,r>"
  PRINT
  PRINT" YOU     COMPUTER"
again:
  c=FIX(RND*3)+1
    IF c=1 THEN c$="P"
    IF c=2 THEN c$="S"
    IF c=3 THEN c$="R"
  ky1: y$=INKEY$ : IF y$="" THEN ky1
    y$=UCASE$(y$)
```

```
   IF y$="Q" THEN END        'exit from the program
      PRINT y$,c$
tie:
   IF y$=c$ THEN SAY TRANSLATE$("TIE") : GOTO again
who.wins:
   IF y$="P" AND c$="S" THEN SAY TRANSLATE$("COMPUTER WINS")
   IF y$="P" AND c$="R" THEN SAY TRANSLATE$("YOU WIN")
   IF y$="S" AND c$="P" THEN SAY TRANSLATE$("YOU WIN")
   IF y$="S" AND c$="R" THEN SAY TRANSLATE$("COMPUTER WINS")
   IF y$="R" AND c$="P" THEN SAY TRANSLATE$("COMPUTER WINS")
   IF y$="R" AND c$="S" THEN SAY TRANSLATE$("YOU WIN")
GOTO again
```

Lesson 15

```
REM >>> Vacation >>>
   CLS : PRINT
   b$=" If you don't like that, try again."
   c$=" Not even two red cents to rub together!"
   a$=" Vacation choosing program"
      PRINT a$ : PRINT
      SAY TRANSLATE$(a$)
   a$=" Pick your vacation by the amount you can spend."
      PRINT a$ : PRINT
      SAY TRANSLATE$(a$)
again:
   RESTORE
   a$=" How many dollars can you spend?"
      PRINT a$ : PRINT
      SAY TRANSLATE$(a$)
   INPUT d
   SAY TRANSLATE$(STR$(d))
   IF d=0 THEN SAY TRANSLATE$(c$) : END
                     READ a$
IF d>1         THEN READ a$
IF d>5         THEN READ a$
IF d>2000000&  THEN READ a$
'etc.
PRINT a$
SAY TRANSLATE$(a$)
IF d<>0 THEN SAY TRANSLATE$(b$) : GOTO again
END
DATA " Flip pennies with your kid sister."
DATA " Spend the afternoon in beautiful Hog Wallow Michigan."
DATA " Enter a pickle eating contest in Scratchy Back Tennessee."
'etc.
DATA " Treat your whole class to a 'round the world trip."
DATA etc.
```

```
REM ↓@#$%^&* Crazy *&^%$#@↓
    CLS : PRINT : RANDOMIZE TIMER
    a$=" What is your name?"
    PRINT a$ : PRINT
    SAY TRANSLATE$(a$)
  INPUT namee$
    CLS :PRINT
    PRINT namee$
  z=FIX(RND*3)+1
    a1$=" Has one brick short of a full load."
    a2$=" Has bats in the attic."
    a3$=" Has not got both oars in the water."
  ON z GOTO 1,2,3
1 PRINT a1$
    SAY TRANSLATE$(namee$+a1$)     :END
2 PRINT a2$
    SAY TRANSLATE$(namee$+a2$)     :END
3 PRINT a3$
    SAY TRANSLATE$(namee$+a3$)     :END
```

Lesson 16

```
REM ^^^ Jumping Name ^^^
  CLS
  RANDOMIZE TIMER
INPUT" Your name";n$
  CLS
FOR s=1 TO 50
    x=RND*60+1 : y=RND*19+1
    LOCATE y,x : PRINT n$;
      FOR t=1 TO 1000:NEXT t
    LOCATE y,x : PRINT STRING$(LEN(n$)," ")
NEXT s


REM +++++ Name X +++++
CLS : INPUT "Your name";na$     : CLS
FOR x=1 TO 22 : LOCATE x,x+25 : PRINT na$ : NEXT x
FOR x=1 TO 22 : LOCATE x,49-x : PRINT na$ : NEXT x
                LOCATE 1,40
```

Lesson 17

```
REM &&&&& Counting By Fives &&&&&
CLS
FOR n=5 TO 100 STEP 5
PRINT n
FOR t=1 TO 1000 : NEXT t
NEXT n


REM +++ Rising Name +++
CLS
INPUT "What is your name? ",na$
CLS
FOR i=21 TO 2 STEP -1
LOCATE i,50-i*2
PRINT na$;
NEXT i
```

Lesson 18

```
REM --- Relations ---
  SAY TRANSLATE$("Relations")
start:
  CLS : PRINT
  PRINT" Enter a relationship like 'father' or 'sister'"
  PRINT" (Enter 'quit' to end program)" : PRINT
  INPUT" Relation";w$
    IF w$="quit" THEN END
    fl=0 : RESTORE
more:
  READ r$ : READ n$
  IF r$="end" THEN GOSUB norel : GOTO start
  IF r$=w$    THEN GOSUB findrel
  GOTO more
findrel:              'Find relative subroutine
  PRINT r$;" ";n$
  SAY TRANSLATE$(r$+", "+n$)
  fl=1 : RETURN
norel:              'No (more) relatives subroutine
  IF fl=0 THEN : SAY TRANSLATE$(" You do not have a "+w$)
  FOR t=1 TO 5000:NEXT t
  RETURN
DATA father,      William
DATA mother,      Jane
DATA sister,      Nancy
DATA sister,      Anne
```

250

```
DATA grandfather, John
DATA grandfather, Mike
DATA grandmother, Sue
DATA grandmother, Constance
DATA uncle,       Harry
DATA aunt,        Vivian
DATA cousin,      Mary
DATA end,         end
```

Lesson 19

```
REM ?????  Data Music ?????
FOR i=1 TO 7
READ a        : a=a*2
SOUND a,10,255
    FOR t=1 TO 200 : NEXT t        ' short space between notes
    SOUND a,1,0
NEXT i
DATA 262,246,220,246,262,262,262,-1
```

Lesson 20

```
REM >>>> Cheers for the Schwartz Creek Trout
READ a,b,j$          : PSET (a,b)
LOCATE 1,1        : PRINT j$ + "                "
sketch:
    READ x        : IF x=999 THEN done
    READ y
    READ j$
LINE - STEP (x,y)
    a=x : b=y
    LOCATE 1,1        : PRINT j$ + "                "
    FOR t=1 TO 5000 : NEXT t
    GOTO sketch
done:
DATA 200,  30      , upper left corner
DATA 200,   0      , draw top
DATA   0,  12      , down a bit
DATA -85,   0      , back to stem
DATA   0, 100      , down to bottom
DATA -30,   0      , across bottom
DATA   0,-100      , up to cross piece
DATA -85,   0      , back toward start
DATA   0, -12      , up to beginning
DATA 999           , end of drawing flag
```

Lesson 21

```
REM >>>>> A Hot Computer >>>>>
  CLS
  SAY TRANSLATE$(" This is your Amiga Speaking          ")
  SAY TRANSLATE$(" I feel a little sick.  Can you help me?  ")
  GOSUB answer
END
answer:
  INPUT a$
  IF a$="y" THEN GOSUB helpful  :  RETURN
  IF a$="n" THEN GOSUB selfish  :  RETURN
                GOSUB neutral    :  RETURN
helpful:
  SAY TRANSLATE$(" Then give me some bytes.  They make me feel
  good. ")
  RETURN
selfish:
  SAY TRANSLATE$(" Well, see if I ever give you another word!")
  RETURN
neutral:
  SAY TRANSLATE$(" Hay!  Make up your mind!                 ")
  RETURN
```

Lesson 22

```
REM ::::: Sinbad's Carpet :::::
  CLS  :  RANDOMIZE TIMER
  SCREEN 2,640,200,4,2
  WINDOW 2,"Sinbad's Carpet",,,2
CALL paintcans
FOR i=10 TO 35        : FOR j=4 TO 14
  COLOR i/3+j/5,1
  LOCATE     j,      i : PRINT "O"
  LOCATE 25-j,      i : PRINT "O"
  LOCATE 25-j,  41-i : PRINT "O"
  LOCATE     j,  41-i : PRINT "O"
NEXT j,i
  FOR t=1 TO 9999      : NEXT t
WINDOW CLOSE 2         :  SCREEN CLOSE 2  :  COLOR 1,0
END

SUB paintcans STATIC
  FOR i=0 TO 15
   READ r : READ g : READ b : READ c$
   PALETTE i,r,g,b
  NEXT i
```

```
      RESTORE
      DATA 1.00, 1.00, 1.00 ,white
      DATA 0.00, 0.00, 0.00 ,black
      DATA 0.40, 0.60, 1.00 ,dark blue
      DATA 0.00, 0.93, 0.87 ,aqua
      DATA 0.47, 0.87, 1.00 ,sky blue
      DATA 0.80, 0.60, 0.53 ,brown
      DATA 0.73, 0.73, 0.73 ,grey
      DATA 0.33, 0.87, 0.00 ,green
      DATA 0.73, 1.00, 0.00 ,lime green
      DATA 1.00, 0.73, 0.00 ,orange
      DATA 0.80, 0.00, 0.93 ,purple
      DATA 1.00, 0.60, 0.67 ,cherry red
      DATA 0.93, 0.20, 0.00 ,red
      DATA 1.00, 0.87, 0.73 ,tan
      DATA 1.00, 0.13, 0.93 ,violet
      DATA 1.00, 1.00, 0.13 ,yellow
 END SUB
```

Lesson 23

```
REM >>>>> School Colors >>>>>
CLS
' Make initials as in the solution A20.2
' We will just make a letter 'o' here
SCREEN 1,640,200,4,2 : WINDOW 2,"School Colors",,16
flash:
CLS
CIRCLE (300,100),90
CIRCLE (300,100),70
PAINT (380,100),1
FOR t=1 TO 3000 : NEXT t
PAINT (380,100),3
GOTO flash
```

Lesson 24

```
REM ((( Months )))
  CLS : PRINT : PRINT : PRINT
  DIM d(12), m$(12)
  FOR I=1 TO 12 : READ d(I)        : NEXT I
  FOR I=1 TO 12 : READ m$(I)       : NEXT I
  INPUT" Month number <1-12>";m    : PRINT
  PRINT" " m$(m);" has";d(m);"days."
DATA  31, 28, 31, 30, 31, 30, 31, 31, 30, 31, 30, 31
DATA Jan,Feb,Mar,Apr,May,Jun,Jul,Aug,Sep,Oct,Nov,Dec
```

Lesson 25

```
REM ***** Cipher Maker *****
  CLS : PRINT
  PRINT" Cipher Making Program"       : PRINT
  PRINT" Enter a sentence for coding:"

  INPUT s$          : s$=s$+" "        : l=LEN(s$)

  FOR i=1 TO l STEP 2
    p$=MID$(s$,i,2)                    'break into pairs
    q$=MID$(p$,2,1)+MID$(p$,1,1)       'reverse letters in pair
    l$=l$+q$                          'assemble output
  NEXT i                               : PRINT

  PRINT" Here is the coded sentence:": PRINT
  PRINT"   ";l$
```

```
REM ????? Question Answerer ?????
  CLS : PRINT
  a$=" Question Answerer"
' Only works for questions with first words = verb.
  PRINT a$ : PRINT
  SAY TRANSLATE$(a$)
  a$=" Enter a question"
  PRINT a$
  SAY TRANSLATE$(a$)
  INPUT q$ : l=LEN(q$)
  SAY TRANSLATE$(q$)
  IF RIGHT$(q$,1)="?" THEN q$=LEFT$(q$,l-1)+"."
verb:
  FOR i=1 TO l            'look for the end of the first word
  c$=MID$(q$,i,1)
  IF c$<>" " THEN spl
```

```
    sl=i : i=l
    spl: NEXT i
    v$=MID$(q$,l,sl)
subject:
    FOR i=sl+1 TO l     'look for the end of the first word
    c$=MID$(q$,i,l)
    IF c$<>" " THEN sp2
    s2=i : i=l
    sp2: NEXT i
    s$=MID$(q$,sl+1,s2-sl)
answer:
    st$=s$+v$+MID$(q$,s2+1,l-s2)
    PRINT
    PRINT "   ";UCASE$(st$)
    SAY TRANSLATE$(st$)




REM ### Pig Latin ###
    CLS : PRINT
  a$=" Pig Latin Program"
    PRINT a$ : SAY TRANSLATE$(a$) : PRINT
    PRINT" Enter 'quit' to end the program." : PRINT
    FOR t=1 TO 9000:NEXT t
start:
    CLS : PRINT
  a$="Give me a word."
    PRINT a$ : SAY TRANSLATE$(a$)
    INPUT w$ : l=LEN(w$)     'get word and its length
  FOR i=1 TO l              'look for first vowel
    v$=MID$(w$,i,l)
      IF v$="a" THEN done
      IF v$="e" THEN done
      IF v$="i" THEN done
      IF v$="o" THEN done
      IF v$="u" THEN done
  NEXT i
done:                     'found it, rearrange the word
  IF i=l THEN l$=w$+"lay" : GOTO sayit 'starts with vowel
    l$=MID$(w$,i,l-i+1)            'get back part of word
    l$=l$+MID$(w$,l,i-1)          'add first syllable to end
    l$=l$+"ay"                    'add "ay"
sayit:
  PRINT "   ";l$ : SAY TRANSLATE$(l$)
    FOR t=1 TO 4000:NEXT t          'pause
  IF w$="quit" THEN fini          'end program?
GOTO start
fini:
  SAY TRANSLATE$("program ends") : END
```

Lesson 27

```
REM ^^^ Leapfrog ^^^
  CLS : PRINT
start:
  INPUT"  Give me a number:",n
    IF n>4999999& THEN PRINT" Too big!" : GOTO start
  b$=""          : CLS
  n$=STR$(n)     : l=LEN(n$)
  n$=MID$(n$,2,l) : l=LEN(n$)
  FOR i=1 TO 61-l
    LOCATE 11,i    : PRINT" "
    LOCATE 11,i+1 : PRINT n$
      FOR t=1 TO 200   : NEXT t
    n$=MID$(n$,2,1-1)+MID$(n$,1,1)
  NEXT i
```

Lesson 28

```
REM /// Alphabetical ///
  CLS : PRINT
  PRINT"  This program arranges the letters of a word in "
  PRINT"  alphabetical order."              : PRINT
  PRINT"  Give me a word:"
  INPUT w$ : l=LEN(w$)  : w$=UCASE$(w$)
  k=1
  FOR i=65 TO 65+26     ' count all A's, then B's, etc.
  FOR j=1 TO l          ' go though letters of word
    g=ASC(MID$(w$,j,1))
    IF g=i THEN h$=h$+CHR$(g)               : k=k+1
  NEXT j,i
  PRINT"  Here it is in alphabetical order:" : PRINT
  PRINT"  ";h$
```

```
REM !@#$%^&* Double Dutch *&^%$#@!
  CLS : PRINT
  SAY TRANSLATE$("double dutch")
again:
  CLS : PRINT
  PRINT" Enter 'quit' to end the program" : PRINT
  a$=" Give me a sentence"
    PRINT a$   : SAY TRANSLATE$(a$)           : PRINT
    INPUT s$   : IF s$="quit" THEN END
    ss$=""
  FOR i=1 TO LEN(s$)
    l$=MID$(s$,i,1)
      IF l$="a" THEN l$="uu"
      IF l$="e" THEN l$="oo"
      IF l$="i" THEN l$="aa"
      IF l$="o" THEN l$="ii"
      IF l$="u" THEN l$="ee"
    ss$=ss$+l$
  NEXT i
  a$="Here it is in Double Dutch"
    SAY TRANSLATE$(a$ )
    SAY TRANSLATE$(ss$)
    PRINT ss$
    FOR t=1 TO 9000 : NEXT t
GOTO again
```

Lesson 29

```
REM |||| Silly Sentences ||||
   CLS
   SAY TRANSLATE$("Silly sentences")
   SAY TRANSLATE$("Press the wi key if you want instructions")
   SAY TRANSLATE$("Press the space bar to continue")
   key1: y$=INKEY$ : IF y$="" THEN key1
   IF UCASE$(y$)="Y" THEN GOSUB instructs
again:
getsubject:
   s$="" : CLS              'erase the last sentence
   SAY TRANSLATE$("Somebody enter a subject.")
   GOSUB getphrase
getverb:
   SAY TRANSLATE$("Somebody enter a verb.")
   GOSUB getphrase
getobject:
   SAY TRANSLATE$("Somebody enter an object.")
   GOSUB getphrase
sillysaying:
   SAY TRANSLATE$(s$)
   CLS : PRINT
   PRINT" Press the space bar to continue" : PRINT
   PRINT" Press 'Q' to end the program."
 choice:
   key2: y$=INKEY$ : IF y$="" THEN key2
   IF UCASE$(y$)="Q" THEN END
   GOTO again
getphrase:
   key3: y$=INKEY$  : IF y$="" THEN key3
   IF ASC(y$)=13 THEN s$=s$+" " : RETURN
   s$=s$+y$    : GOTO getphrase
instructs:
 PRINT" Three players enter parts of a sentence."
 PRINT" (No player can see what the others are entering.)":PRINT
 PRINT"   The first player enters a subject."
 PRINT"     (The person doing something.)"              :PRINT
 PRINT"   The second player enters a verb."
 PRINT"     (The action word.)"                         :PRINT
 PRINT"   The third player enters the object."
 PRINT"     (The person or thing to whom the action is done.)"
   FOR t=1 TO 20000:NEXT t
RETURN
```

Lesson 30

```
REM === Ain't got no ===
  CLS : PRINT
  PRINT" Enter 'quit' to end the program" : PRINT
getsentence:
  PRINT" Enter a sentence.  No punctuation except appostrophe."
  PRINT
  INPUT s$  : s$=UCASE$(s$) : IF s$="QUIT" THEN END
  s$=s$+" " : l=LEN(s$)
lookfornegs:
        ' nw is the number of negative words in the sentence
        ' sb is the beginning letter place of the word
        ' se is the end place
  nw=0 : sb=1 : se=1
cutwords:                       'run through the sentence
  FOR i=1 TO l
    l$=MID$(s$,i,1)        'look for the space at a word end
    IF l$=" " THEN sb=se : se=i+1 : GOSUB negword
  NEXT i
printresult:                            : PRINT
  IF nw=0 THEN PRINT"  No negative words."
  IF nw=1 THEN PRINT"  A negative sentence."
  IF nw=2 THEN PRINT"  A double negative."
  IF nw>2 THEN PRINT"  Hard to understand!"
    FOR t=1 TO 5000:NEXT t             : PRINT
  GOTO getsentence
negword:
    lw=se-sb-1
    w$=MID$(s$,sb,lw)
 nextword:
    READ nw$
        IF nw$="END" THEN RESTORE  : RETURN
        IF w$=nw$ THEN nw=nw+1
 GOTO nextword
listofwords:
  DATA NO,NOT,NEVER,NONE,NOTHING,DON'T,DOESN'T,AREN'T
  DATA AIN'T,ISN'T,DIDN'T,HAVEN'T,HASN'T,HADN'T
  DATA WOULDN'T,COULDN'T,SHOULDN'T,END
trythese:
'I like junk food.
'I don't eat junk food.
'I don't eat no junk food.
'I don't never eat no junk food.
```

Lesson 32

```
REM +++++ A Jillion +++++
  CLS : PRINT
  SAY TRANSLATE$("Here is a big big number.")
  FOR k=1 TO 18          'do 18 lines
    FOR i=1 TO 15        '15 triplets per line
      FOR j=1 TO 3       'three numbers per triplet
        d=FIX(RND*1Ø)+48 : d$=CHR$(d)
        PRINT d$;
      NEXT j
      IF k=18 AND i=15 AND j=4 THEN skip
      PRINT",";               'put comma after triplet
      skip:
    NEXT i
  PRINT                       'skip to next line
  NEXT k
  SAY TRANSLATE$("How big is it?")


REM ????? Code - Decode ?????
  CLS : PRINT
  a$="abcdefghijklmnopqrstuvwxyz"
  b$=a$
shorten.password:
  PRINT" Input the password":PRINT
  INPUT pw$
  f$=LEFT$(pw$,1)
      FOR   i=2 TO LEN(pw$) : l1$=MID$(pw$,i,1)
        FOR j=1 TO LEN(f$ ) : l2$=MID$(f$, j,1)
          IF l1$=l2$ THEN jump
        NEXT j : f$=f$+l1$
jump: NEXT i    : pw$=f$
  PRINT" The shortened password is"
  PRINT : PRINT"   ";pw$
remove.letters:
  FOR   j=1 TO LEN(pw$)
                        l2$=MID$(pw$,j,1)
      IF l2$=LEFT$(a$,1) THEN a$=MID$( a$,2  ) : GOTO jmp2
    FOR i=1 TO LEN(a$ )
                        l1$=MID$(a$, i,1)
      IF l1$=l2$        THEN a$=LEFT$(a$,i-1)+MID$(a$,i+1)
    NEXT i
    jmp2: NEXT j
form.cipher.alphabet:
  a$=pw$+a$    : PRINT
  PRINT" Alphabets:"
  PRINT               TAB(23);"plain"
```

260

```basic
    PRINT" ";b$
    PRINT" ";a$
    PRINT                TAB(23);"cipher" : PRINT
choice:
    PRINT" Code or decode? <c/d> "
    ky1: y$=INKEY$ : IF y$="" THEN ky1
    IF UCASE$(y$)="C" THEN code
    IF UCASE$(y$)="D" THEN decode
    GOTO ky1
code:
    PRINT
    PRINT" Input message to be coded:"
    ky2: l$=INKEY$  : IF l$="" THEN ky2
      l$=UCASE$(l$) : l=ASC(l$)  : IF l=13   THEN code1
      PRINT l$;      : cl$=l$       ' default is no change
      IF l>64 AND l<87 THEN  cl$=MID$(a$,l-64,1)
      ct$=ct$+cl$
    GOTO ky2
    code1:
    PRINT : PRINT ct$
    GOTO finish
decode:
    PRINT
    PRINT" Input message to be decoded:"
    ky3: l$=INKEY$  : IF l$="" THEN ky3
      l$=UCASE$(l$) : l=ASC(l$)  : IF l=13   THEN out
      PRINT l$;      : cl$=l$       ' default = won't find letter
      FOR i=1 TO 26 ' is letter in cipher alphabet?
        IF l$=UCASE$(MID$(a$,i,1)) THEN cl$=MID$(b$,i,1)
      NEXT i
      ct$=ct$+cl$
    GOTO ky3
 out:
    PRINT
    PRINT ct$
finish:
    END
```

Index of Reserved Words

Topical Index

COMPUTE! Books

Ask your retailer for these **COMPUTE! Books** or order directly from **COMPUTE!**.
Call toll free (in US) **1-800-346-6767** (in NY 212-887-8525) or write COMPUTE! Books, P.O. Box 5038, F.D.R. Station, New York, NY 10150.

Quantity	Title	Price*	Total
_____	COMPUTE!'s Beginner's Guide to the Amiga (025-4)	**$16.95**	_____
_____	COMPUTE!'s AmigaDOS Reference Guide (047-5)	**$14.95**	_____
_____	Elementary Amiga BASIC (041-6)	**$14.95**	_____
_____	COMPUTE!'s Amiga Programmer's Guide (028-9)	**$16.95**	_____
_____	COMPUTE!'s Kids and the Amiga (048-3)	**$14.95**	_____
_____	Inside Amiga Graphics (040-8)	**$16.95**	_____
_____	Advanced Amiga BASIC (045-9)	**$16.95**	_____

*Add $2.00 per book for shipping and handling.
Outside US add $5.00 air mail or $2.00 surface mail.

NC residents add 4.5% sales tax _____
Shipping & handling: $2.00/book _____
Total payment _____

All orders must be prepaid (check, charge, or money order).
All payments must be in US funds.
NC residents add 4.5% sales tax.
☐ Payment enclosed.
Charge   ☐ Visa   ☐ MasterCard   ☐ American Express

Acct. No._____ Exp. Date_____

Name_____

Address_____

City_____ State _____ Zip_____

*Allow 4–5 weeks for delivery.
Prices and availability subject to change.
Current catalog available upon request.

COMPUTE! Books

Ask your retailer for these **COMPUTE! Books** or order directly from **COMPUTE!**.

Call toll free (in US) **800-346-6767** (in NY 212-887-8525) or write COMPUTE! Books, P.O. Box 5038, F.D.R. Station, New York, NY 10150

Quantity	Title	Price*	Total
_____	Machine Language for Beginners (11-6)	$14.95	_____
_____	The Second Book of Machine Language (53-1)	$14.95	_____
_____	COMPUTE!'s Guide to Adventure Games (67-1)	$12.95	_____
_____	Computing Together: A Parents & Teachers Guide to Computing with Young Children (51-5)	$12.95	_____
_____	COMPUTE!'s Personal Telecomputing (47-7)	$12.95	_____
_____	BASIC Programs for Small Computers (38-8)	$12.95	_____
_____	Programmer's Reference Guide to the Color Computer (19-1)	$12.95	_____
_____	Home Energy Applications (10-8)	$14.95	_____
	The Home Computer Wars: An Insider's Account of Commodore and Jack Tramiel		
_____	Hardback (75-2)	$16.95	_____
_____	Paperback (78-7)	$ 9.95	_____
_____	The Book of BASIC (61-2)	$12.95	_____
_____	The Greatest Games: The 93 Best Computer Games of all Time (95-7)	$ 9.95	
_____	Investment Management with Your Personal Computer (005)	$14.95	
_____	40 Great Flight Simulator Adventures (022)	$ 9.95	_____
_____	40 More Great Flight Simulator Adventures (043-2)	$ 9.95	_____
_____	100 Programs for Business and Professional Use (017-3)	$24.95	_____
_____	From BASIC to C (026)	$16.95	_____
_____	The Turbo Pascal Handbook (037)	$14.95	_____
_____	Electronic Computer Projects (052-1)	$ 9.95	_____

* Add $2.00 per book for shipping and handling.
Outside US add $5.00 air mail or $2.00 surface mail.

NC residents add 4.5% sales tax. _____
Shipping & handling: $2.00/book _____
Total payment _____

All orders must be prepaid (check, charge, or money order).
All payments must be in US funds.
☐ Payment enclosed.
Charge ☐ Visa ☐ MasterCard ☐ American Express

Acct. No. _____ Exp. Date _____
                                                                    (Required)
Name _____

Address _____

City _____ State _____ Zip _____

*Allow 4–5 weeks for delivery.
Prices and availability subject to change.
Current catalog available upon request.

If you've enjoyed the articles in this book, you'll find the same style and quality in every monthly issue of **COMPUTE!** Magazine. Use this form to order your subscription to **COMPUTE!**.

For Fastest Service
Call Our **Toll-Free** US Order Line
1-800-247-5470
In IA call 1-800-532-1272

COMPUTE!
P.O. Box 10954
Des Moines, IA 50340

My computer is:
☐ Commodore 64 or 128 ☐ TI-99/4A ☐ IBM PC or PCjr ☐ VIC-20
☐ Apple ☐ Atari ☐ Amiga ☐ Other _____
☐ Don't yet have one...

☐ $24 One Year US Subscription
☐ $45 Two Year US Subscription
☐ $65 Three Year US Subscription
Subscription rates outside the US:

☐ $30 Canada and Foreign Surface Mail
☐ $65 Foreign Air Delivery

Name _____

Address _____

City _____ State _____ Zip _____

Country _____

Payment must be in US funds drawn on a US bank, international money order, or charge card.
☐ Payment Enclosed ☐ Visa
☐ MasterCard ☐ American Express

Acct. No. _____ Expires ____ / ____
                                              (Required)

Your subscription will begin with the next available issue. Please allow 4–6 weeks for delivery of first issue. Subscription prices subject to change at any time.